EMERGE TO GREATNESS

7 Shifts to Transform Your Mindset
and Reach Your Highest Potential

Haynie Smith

ALL RIGHTS RESERVED. No part of this book or its associated ancillary materials may be reproduced or transmitted in any form or by any means, electronic or mechanical, including photocopying, recording, or by any information storage or retrieval system without permission of publisher.

PUBLISHED BY: Emerging Music Entertainment, LLC
P.O.BOX 510492 Milwaukee, Wisconsin 53203

DISCLAIMER AND/OR LEGAL NOTICES

While all attempts have been made to verify information provided in this book and its ancillary materials, neither the author nor publisher assumes responsibility for errors, inaccuracies, or omissions and is not responsible for any monetary loss in any matter. If advice concerning legal, financial, accounting or related matters is needed, the services of a qualified professional should be sought. This book or its associated ancillary materials, including verbal and written training, is not intended for use as a source of legal, financial, or accounting advice. You should be aware of the various laws governing business transactions or other business practices in your state. The information contained in this book is strictly for educational purposes. Therefore, if you wish to apply ideas contained in this book, you are taking full responsibility for your actions. There is no guarantee or promise, expressed or implied, that you will earn any money using the strategies, concepts, techniques, exercises and ideas in the book.

STANDARD EARNINGS AND INCOME DISCLAIMER

With respect to the reliability, accuracy, timeliness, usefulness, adequacy, completeness, and/or suitability of information provided in this book, Emerging Music Entertainment, LLC. its partners' associates, affiliates, consultants, and/or presenters make no warranties, guarantees, representations, or claims of any kind. Participants' results will vary depending on many factors. All claims or representations as to income earning are not considered as average earnings. All products and services are for educational and informational purposes only. Check with your accountant, attorney, or professional advisor before acting on this or any information. By continuing with reading this book, you agree that Emerging Music Entertainment, LLC. is not responsible for the success or failure of your personal, business, or financial decisions relating to any information.

PRINTED IN THE UNITED STATES OF AMERICA | FIRST EDITION

© All Rights Reserved. Copyright 2023. Emerging Music Entertainment LLC.

Dedication

☙

I dedicate this book to anyone who has broken barriers to create opportunities for self and others, those seeking to win against their lesser self and adversity, and those who believe in Human Revolution.

"I embraced adversity as opportunity; and I know it's within my power to take anything and make it be the best thing that ever happened."

- Will Smith, *Best Shape of My Life*

Table of Contents

☙

Dedication	3
Preface	11

Mindshift One
Declutter Your Mind!

The Primary Causes of Mental Clutter	14
Declutter Your Home and Work Environments First	14
Consider How Much the People in Your Life Add and Detract from It	17
Evaluate the Distractions You Face in Your Life Each Day	19
Dealing with Thought-Based Clutter	21
The Breath is the Key	24
Clarify Your Purpose	30

Mindshift Two
Understanding Fear and How to Break Through

The Difference Between Fears and Phobias	35
Is Fear the Mind Killer?	36
Fear is an Emotion	39
How to Control My Fear?	41
Fear Analysis Questions	50
Change Your Biology	52
Identify Your Fears	52
Focus on What You Can Control	54
I Replace Fear With Faith	60
Self-Reflection Questions	61

Mindshift Three
Be Mindful of Your Thoughts, Make Changes if Necessary

When You Feel Afraid	65
When You're Consumed with Negativity	67
Deal Quickly with Your Negative Thoughts	69
When You Lack Confidence	70
When You Wish to Get a Good Night's Sleep	72
When You Want to Be More Productive	74
When Your Anger is Ruling Your Life	76

When Determining If You Should End an Unhealthy Relationship	78
When You Want to Feel Comfortable Being Alone	80

Mindshift Four
Believe in You, Practice Self-Reliance!

Pitfalls of Dependence	84
Benefits of Self-Reliance	85
Health	86
Individuality	89
Mental Toughness	91
Relationships	95
Financial Stability	96

Mindshift Five
Rebuild Your Self-Esteem

Apply Yourself at Work to Increase Your Self-Esteem	100
Use Your Cognitions to Build a Positive View of Yourself	102
Do Some Housecleaning—Physically and Emotionally	105
Immerse Yourself in Hobbies and Activities You Love	107
Concentrate on Being a Great Partner or Parent	109
Recognize Physical Well-Being is Intimately Connected with Your Self-Esteem	111
Rejoice in Your Uniqueness	112

Mindshift Six
Tap Into Your Intuition

What is Intuition?	116
The Value of Intuition	118
Obstacles to Intuition	120
Intuition-Boosting Exercises	123
Using Your Intuition to Make Effective Decisions	129
Using Your Intuition to Find Your Purpose in Life	131
Tips to Use Daily to Enhance Your Intuition	134

Mindshift Seven
Master Your Day

Optimizing Productivity with Time and Space	138
Focused Task Management	142
Prioritizing Daily Tasks	146
Pay Attention to Your Time	148
Setting Up Your Daily System	151
Set a Schedule, Stick to It	155
Final Encouragement You Are on Your Way to Your Best You	165

"Look through the clutter, you already have the gift!"

Trolls: Holiday in Harmony

Preface

☙

By design, I wasn't supposed to make it. I wasn't supposed to be here. Everything in my environment, my history, and seemingly what was to be my future—all was supposed to lead to my inevitable defeat and premature demise, first spiritually, then physically. Growing up in Milwaukee, Wisconsin as a Black male made me a target for any and everything that could take me out. I grew up in the most segregated city in America, my young mother was unexpectedly widowed when I was four years old, and I went to a school that literally didn't teach me anything. This is not to mention all the horrific and tragic karma I saw play out before my eyes in my community and within my own family. All I saw around me was untapped potential, and I was determined to break that cycle. *This all will end with me. I will shift the momentum of my lineage.*

I realized I had to start assessing my own mental health, which was not in very good shape. I began by writing down the victories and failures of my life and the lives of others. I analyzed the cause-and-effect relationship of these victories and failures. I found that, interestingly enough, there was only one reason for both my failures and successes:

my mindset. I discovered that I was in a chronically poisonous mindset that inevitably led to my ultimate failure. When I consciously shifted that mindset, somehow, I was victorious. As simple as this may seem, it was genuinely world-changing for me.

To test out this theory, I applied it to the lives of people whom I admire and to the lives of people who were really suffering. Again, everything came down to their mindsets. After facing and overcoming the ugly reality of my mental health challenges by learning about and applying mindset shifts, or "Mindshifts," successfully, I quickly developed a passion for helping people break through their own obstacles. I found that in helping others, I was also learning more about myself in the process.

Since my awareness of the interconnectedness of all people is at the forefront of everything I do, I really had no choice but to do my best to share what has helped me so profoundly with as many people as I can. These seven powerful Mindshifts jump-started the process of breaking through many of my challenges. I share these with you with complete confidence that you, too, can implement these Mindshifts in your own life in ways that make the most sense to you and find even greater success and fulfillment throughout your life journey.

The internal work is far from finished. Even while writing this book, I experienced many obstacles in the process of completing this book. I actively overcame my fear and worry about mistakes, consciously de-cluttered my mind and environment, took MANY breaks, and frankly rebuilt my self-esteem. I had to hone in on strengthening my mindset to believe in my ability to make my life what I want and to take risks even when scared. Cause and effect is an absolute law. I've shifted my mindset and have shifted the trajectory of my life. Now it's your turn!

Mindshift One
Declutter Your Mind!

❧

The word decluttering doesn't just apply to housekeeping. In a household setting, decluttering refers to cleaning, general tidying, and eliminating things from the home that have become useless or obsolete.

The same concept can be applied to your mind. *It's the process of lowering the burden on your mind by eliminating unnecessary worry and thoughts.* This can be accomplished by making changes to your life and your thought processes. Though clutter is always caused by your mental processes, external events can serve as triggers.

Eliminating the triggers is a powerful way to declutter your mind.

But you also have ineffective habits for dealing with stress, boredom, and uncertainty. Excessive thinking can be another form of mental clutter. It uses valuable resources and drains your ability to focus.

Your environment is another possible source of mental clutter. A cluttered environment is not conducive to a calm and relaxed attitude. The people in your life can also clutter your mind.

It is important to address every possible cause.

"When we clear the physical clutter from our lives, we literally make way for inspiration and good, orderly direction to enter."

- Julia Cameron

The Primary Causes of Mental Clutter

Your environment includes your home and work environments. You spend most of your time in one of these two places. ***Avoid underestimating the impact your environment can have on your mental clutter.*** Removing environmental clutter can have a positive effect on the clutter between your ears.

Cleaning your office won't trigger feelings of sentimentality, but decluttering your home will. The most important criteria when deciding whether or not to keep an item are:

- Do I love it?
- Do I need it?

If the answer is "no" to both questions, get rid of it. Sentimentality is a trap. There's no reason to keep your plastic prom corsage or tux from 1999 if it spends its entire life in a box or in the closet. However, there are worse offenses in the universe. Just be aware of the tendency of sentimentality to contribute to your environmental and mental clutter.

Declutter Your Home and Work Environments First

1. **Tackle one room at a time.** Attempting to take on too much at once will not only lead to failure, but you'll also increase your level of mental clutter. Let's not lose ground before we even get started!

- A quick declutter is enough. Assuming you're not a hoarder, each room shouldn't take more than 30 minutes to clear away the visual clutter.

2. **Start at the top and work your way down.** Look at anything hanging on the walls. ***Do you love it? Do you need it?*** If the answer to both questions is "no," sell it, throw it away, or give it away. Regardless of which option you choose, do it quickly.

3. **Go through any closets, drawers, and shelves.** Repeat the same process. If you don't need it or love it, get rid of it.

4. **Finish the room.** Consider the furniture, books, items under the bed, your clothes, and so on. Every single item should be considered for elimination. Be ruthless. ***You don't use 90% of your possessions. You won't miss them.***

5. **Complete the rest of the house.** Include the garage, refrigerator, under the sinks, and every other location. Do you have more towels than you need? Do you have towels that are so threadbare that you avoid using them? Shoes that hurt your feet? Clothes that don't fit? Paper you never shredded? Get rid of it all. Anything that stays in the house should be important to you or your life.

   - *Focus on one room per day.* It's not necessary to spend a lot of time on each room if you move quickly and don't spend 10 minutes on each item. If you're not positive about keeping it, let it go.

   - *Remember your car.* In fact, you can declutter your car every time you fill your gas tank. Don't just stand there watching the numbers increase on the gas pump! Declutter your car while you wait.

6. **Address your work environment.** Your work environment might consist of a desk and cubicle or an office. Or you might be responsible for an entire facility. Declutter whatever falls under your responsibility. Pay special attention to your desk and old files. Take the appropriate actions.

7. **Remember your digital environment.** This can be the most tedious part of your decluttering efforts. It might take the better part of a Saturday to complete.

   - **Computer.** This includes your computer desktop and all your files. Eliminate everything you don't need. Organize files and icons as needed. Consider defragmenting your hard drive after you're done. Declutter your work computer, too.

   - **Email.** How many emails do you have that you don't need? Remember to spend time on all your email accounts.

   - **Phone.** Delete old text messages. Delete apps you no longer use. Update your apps as needed.

8. **Evaluate how you feel.** After all of these unnecessary items are out of your house and workspace, notice how you feel. You likely feel happier, lighter, and less burdened. It's a good feeling. Remember it. And remember what caused it – less things in your life, not more.

It might seem counterintuitive to address your environment when your challenge is more psychological in nature. ***However, your environment can influence the amount of stress and anxiety you experience.*** This can trigger mental habits that create the mental clutter you're trying to relieve.

"I'm quite an untidy person in a lot of ways. But order makes me happy. I have to have a clear desk and a tidy desktop, with as few visual distractions as possible. I don't mind sound distractions, but visual ones freak me out."

- Joanne Harris

Consider How Much the People in Your Life Add and Detract from It

There are certain people who are hard to eliminate from your life. Your children are one example. No matter how old your children may be, the bond between parent and child is strong. However, there are situations that can justify eliminating adult children or your parents from your life. **Not everyone has a place in your life.**

Your life is sacred. Be careful whom you choose to include.

1. **Which people are a source of negativity?** These people aren't negative about your life. They're negative about life in general. These are the people who are pessimistic, complain about everything, and suck the life out of you every time you see them. Ask yourself why you keep them around.

2. **Consider the toxic people in your life.** Toxic people get in your way. They're the people who get in the way of you reaching your goals. They're discouraging and sabotaging. For some reason, they feel better if you don't better yourself.

   - *It's rare to have people who truly want to see you excel.* However, that's no reason to tolerate those who intentionally become obstacles in your life. Show them the door and lock it. These kinds of people are detrimental not only to your progress, but to your overall health as well.

- *If it's a close friend or family member, first have a frank discussion.* If that fails to have an effect, then show them the door.

3. **Friends from another time.** It might be an old college friend or a co-worker from 20 years ago. Do you have anything in common besides the past? How much enjoyment do you receive from them? Think about it and make the necessary adjustments.

4. **Unfamiliar social media pals.** You know these people. They're Facebook "friends" who are actually friends of friends of friends. Do you need to see the pictures of their shoes, clothes, or flashy money?

   - *If you're using social media to promote your business, the more the merrier.* Otherwise, make the necessary cuts.

5. **Think about the people at work.** You have fewer options here. You might be able to eliminate those troubling people who work for you, but even that's not easy in today's day and age. You can find another position within the same company or at another company.

Not everyone deserves to be part of your life. As far as anyone knows for certain, you only get one chance. **Ensure you're not allowing the people around you to lower your life force.** Please, eliminate those people who are unnecessary or whom you do not love. Make room for people who will contribute to your life and happiness.

> *"As important as it is to learn how to deal with different kinds of people, truly toxic people will never be worth your time and energy - and they take a lot of each. Toxic people create unnecessary complexity, strife, and, worst of all, stress."*
>
> *- Travis Bradberry*

Evaluate the Distractions You Face in Your Life Each Day

Distractions can be clutter in themselves. ***Distractions can also be contributors to clutter by diverting your attention from what's important and allowing clutter to grow.*** Procrastination is a self-created phenomenon that everyone faces.

You never feel good while procrastinating. The work that you're avoiding is still hanging over your head. ***No distraction is enough to completely eliminate that nagging feeling.*** You continue to check the time and shift your attention back and forth between the distraction and the work you should be doing. The result is mental clutter.

Some distractions aren't all that distracting. They just happen to be a more enjoyable option than the work you should be doing. However, some distractions are highly distracting in their own right.

1. **How do you waste time?** Forget about procrastinating. If you have nothing pressing on your schedule, how do you waste time? Make a list. A few popular culprits include:

    - Internet
    - TV
    - Cell phone-related activities
    - Video games
    - Shopping
    - Mindless chatting with friends
    - These are likely the same ways you spend your time while procrastinating.

    Include more ways you waste your time below.

2. **Consider the cost of losing that time.** Even if you only waste one hour per day, and it is likely much more than that, that's 365 hours per year. That is over nine 40-hour work weeks. That is over two months! What else could you do with that hour?

    - Exercise
    - Build a blog
    - Take a college course
    - Make new friends
    - Write a book
    - Learn a language
    - Learn an instrument

3. **Make a list before bed.** Prepare a list of the most important three to five tasks you must do the following day. Ensure that at least half of your list are items that will move your life forward in some way.

4. **Understand why those items are important.** Understand the benefit you are gaining by taking these actions.

5. **Reduce each task to the necessary steps.** Tasks that are too big or too poorly defined encourage procrastination.

6. **Reduce your distractions.** Remove any distractions from your environment. Turn off your phone. Turn off the internet. Unplug the television. Shut the door to your office. Lock yourself in the basement or bare closet if you must.

7. **Set a timer.** Unless you have been meditating in a cave for the last 10 years, you cannot expect yourself to be able to concentrate for eight hours straight. Use a timer to create time boundaries. ***Most of us can concentrate for 30-60 min-***

utes at a time. Then take a break for 5-10 minutes and get back after it.

Distractions are everywhere. Some of us are naturally better at ignoring distractions than others. ***Use your time to the best of your ability by reducing the distractions in your life.*** You are then in a stronger position to avoid procrastination.

Consider that the worst procrastinators you know are struggling the most with life. **Procrastination is perhaps the greatest fertilizer for mental clutter.**

> *"Elegance is achieved when all that is superfluous has been discarded and the human being discovers simplicity and concentration: the simpler and more sober the posture, the more beautiful it will be."*
>
> **- Paulo Coelho**

Dealing with Thought-Based Clutter

Your thoughts are the genesis of mental clutter. This is where it all starts. ***Get control of your thoughts, and your mental clutter will be tamed.*** This is a major task, and not for the faint-hearted! It can be done, though.

There are several things that affect your thoughts. These include:

- Mental habits
- Everyday stress
- Making decisions, especially when there are too many options
- Unfinished business

Mental habits

Like your actions, many of your thoughts are habitual. You think about the same past experiences over and over. You daydream about the same imagined future over and over. These thoughts may be positive or negative, but they still contribute to mental clutter.

There are other mental habits that provide little benefit:

- Guilt
- Worry
- Regret
- Comparing yourself to others
- Gaining self-esteem by pleasing others
- Mentally checking out when faced with stressful situations
- Worry what others think of you
- Expecting the worst
- Thinking about the past and the future

Contemplate whether you struggle with any of these negative mental habits.

Everyday Stress

This is a big one. ***Your mind fills with clutter as your stress level increases.*** Your thoughts become less controlled and more negative. It is not surprising that many serious mental health issues are often precipitated by stressful events. The level of stress that you face each day is relevant to the amount of mental clutter you have.

It is often the accumulation of little things that have a significant impact. It is traffic, late bills, a runny nose, an annoyed spouse, and a broken shoelace that can send your brain into a tailspin. Too many smaller stressors can be just as stressful as large stressors.

> *"The greatest weapon against stress is our ability to choose one thought over another."*
>
> **- William James**

Decisions

Making a lot of decisions can really wear you out and create mental clutter. There's a reason why Steve Jobs, Barack Obama, and Albert Einstein limited their daily wardrobes to just a few items – the elimination of choice.

When you're faced with too many decisions, mental clutter grows. **Studies also show that making decisions decreases your ability to make additional decisions.** Eliminate as many possible decisions as you can each day.

This is one good thing about habits. Habits eliminate the need to make a choice. Stick with the same healthy breakfast and take the same route to work each day. *Use habits to your advantage and save your decision-making muscles for important decisions.*

Unfinished Business

Often the result of procrastination or indecisiveness, unfinished business takes up valuable mental space. It's the phone call you need to make. It's cleaning out your storage unit. It's finishing your taxes. It's getting the oil changed in your car.

These things can seem trivial in the short-term, but there's a price to be paid each day. Notice how much better you feel when you complete these responsibilities.

> *"Being in control of your life and having realistic expectations about your day-to-day challenges are the keys to stress management, which is perhaps the most important ingredient to living a happy, healthy and rewarding life."*
>
> *- Marilu Henner*

There's good news. **All of your mental clutter is ultimately self-induced.** Fortunately, that means that your mental clutter is under your control. It also means that you don't have anyone to blame besides yourself.

The Breath is the Key

The process of breathing is pretty amazing. It is the only bodily function that you can consciously control or have done for you automatically. You can breathe more deeply or more shallowly on command. Fast or slower isn't a problem either. On the other hand, you can forget all about breathing, and it still happens.

An adult at rest takes roughly 20 breaths per minute. That's over 28,000 breaths per day. Most of those breaths happened without any intention on your part. You weren't even aware of at least 99% of them.

Some might argue this arrangement is necessary for speech to occur. Maybe it's more than that. Maybe it's the secret to managing your thoughts!

There are two ways breathing benefits mental clutter:

1. **Changing your breathing can change your physiology.** Try breathing faster for a minute and notice how you feel. Now breathe very deeply for a minute and notice the changes. Changes to your breathing change your physiology. Changing your physiology can change your thoughts and your focus.

2. **Focusing on your breath can keep your mind in the present moment.** *Your breath is your thread to the present.* No matter how distracted you are by your thoughts, focusing on your breath can bring you back to reality.

Breathing doesn't seem too exciting, but it is a powerful tool. What could be simpler? However, there is a skill component to using your breath in your clutter-reducing efforts. It will take time and patience to develop fully.

Use your breath to alter your physiology:

1. **Find a quiet place, if possible.** If you're at work, close your office door or head for the bathroom. The more solitude you can find, the better. *However, the technique will work anywhere, especially with practice.*
2. **Take a comfortable position.** Seated is best. Ideally, you can assume a position that you can maintain for at least five minutes without moving.
3. **Inhale slowly and deeply through your nose.** Allow your stomach to expand. You're not trying to breathe so deeply that you feel pain. Just take a full breath. Feel the air pass by the tips of your nostrils. Then relax and allow the air to expel naturally.
   - Avoid overcomplicating the technique. Full, slow, and easy breaths are the objective. Paying attention to your breath for just 5-10 minutes can be enough to feel a significant reduction in both your stress level and mental clutter.

This simple technique can be used anytime you're feeling stressed or your mind is cluttered. This falls short of true meditation, but you can receive many of the same benefits. ***This focused breathing technique can be used in the car, during a meeting, or any time you need to regain control of your racing brain.***

Meditation is the next logical step. Meditation is like focused breathing on steroids. It's more than just a quick-fix. It can literally transform your life.

There are many scientifically proven benefits to meditation:

1. **Meditation decreases depression.** Meditation has been shown to reduce obsession with one's discomfort and distress. In other words, you spend less time thinking about your challenges. This leads to a lower incidence of depression.

2. **Meditation increases the ability to regulate your mood.** We have some control over our moods, just not as much as we'd like. You can probably think of someone in your life that regulates their moods very poorly. You never know what you're going to face when you see them. Meditation enhances the ability to manage your moods.

3. **It decreases anxiety.** ***Both emotional and physical stress markers are reduced in those who meditate.***

4. **It increases the ability to focus and work under stress.** This can be one of the biggest benefits to those who meditate to declutter their mind.

    - It's not easy to sit still for an extended period of time and maintain your focus. As that ability grows, you can apply it to other areas in your life.

5. **Meditation increases resilience.** You'll be overwhelmed less frequently and find it easier to continue during times of stress.

There is a nearly endless list of the benefits provided by regular meditation. But it's obvious that meditation is a great tool to declutter your mind. *When you're in a better mood, feel less stress, and are able to focus, your mind is less cluttered!*

Everyone has at least a vague idea of what is involved in meditation, but the details are a little fuzzy for most. This is understandable, as there are many types of meditation.

Mindfulness meditation is an excellent choice for those who want to declutter their thoughts. This type of meditation is based on observations. You're not thinking, evaluating, or interpreting your thoughts. There's no judging involved.

You're just paying attention in a particular way.

Since it's just a particular way of paying attention, you can do it during a variety of activities. These include:

- Driving
- Eating
- Cleaning
- Showering
- Mowing the lawn
- Using the phone

While some forms of meditation attempt to limit thoughts, mindfulness meditation simply notices the thoughts that appear. This is great for beginners, because limiting your thoughts is very challenging!

Mindfulness meditation is a simple, yet challenging, process:

1. **Assume a comfortable seated position.** A chair is fine. The floor is also an acceptable option. Comfort and support are key.

2. **Become aware of your surroundings.** Notice the temperature of the room. Notice the physical sensations of your feet, hands, back, neck and every other part of your body. Notice what you can see in the room. What do you hear?

   - *Avoid judging anything.* Even labeling isn't permitted. For example, you might notice a blue piece of artwork on the wall. It's not appropriate to say to yourself, "Wow, that's kind of ugly." Saying something positive about the artwork isn't any better! Avoid even saying to yourself, "Blue artwork."

   - *Keep your thoughts limited to what you can see, hear, and smell.* If you hear a dog bark and remind yourself that you don't like that dog, you're not being mindful. Just notice the dog barking.

   - *It's surprising how relaxing this can be.* Just notice and keep your brain's big mouth shut. ***Do this for five minutes.***

3. **Turn your attention to your breath.** Feel the breath throughout your body. Start at the nostrils and notice the movement and sensations of your chest and abdomen. Keep your attention on the part of your body where the breath is most easily felt.

   - *Continue this until the end of the meditation.* Strive for a total time of at least 20 minutes.

4. **Notice your thoughts.** Invariably, it won't take too long before you realize that you're thinking about your meeting tomorrow or your best friend from third grade. That's okay. Again, avoid labeling your thoughts. The following are unacceptable:

- *"That's a weird thought."*
- *"Why did I think about that?"*
- *"What's wrong with me?"*
- *"I must be nuts."*

As with the sights and sounds in your environment, notice the thought without taking the next step of judging or labeling.

5. **Return your awareness to your breath.** It's that simple.

Over time, you'll find that your thoughts, judgments, and tendency to label things will decrease. The result is a decrease in your mental clutter.

Consider how much mental noise you generate each day. Imagine you are walking from your car into work. It's 90 degrees outside. Think about the conversation you might have with yourself.

- *"It sure is hot today."*
- *"I wonder what the news predicted for the high today."*
- *"It's okay. We'll be in the air conditioning soon."*
- *"That's a nice tree. I wonder how old it is?"*

Labeling things in your environment is a habit that accomplishes little. You don't need to tell yourself it's hot outside. You already know! You don't need to comfort yourself by telling yourself that you'll be in the cool a/c in just a minute. You already know! You can see the tree just fine, too.

Meditation helps to quiet this unnecessary mental noise. When you stop generating mental chatter, you can deal with the real clutter in your life much more effectively. You'll be amazed at how capable you really are.

> *"Meditation is difficult for many people because their thoughts are always on some distant object or place."*
>
> *- Wayne Dyer*

Clarify Your Purpose

> *"There is a plan and a purpose, a value to every life, no matter what its location, age, gender or disability."*
>
> *- Sharron Angle*

Indecisiveness can be the result of a lack of clarity. ***If you're unclear about your values and your goals, you lack purpose.*** You've been developing your values since childhood. They undergo modification as you age and develop new perspectives on life.

But you've probably never really given your values much thought. Now is the time to take a hard look.

Determine your values and make easier, more congruent decisions:

1. **Determine what's most important to you in life.** Ask yourself the question and see what pops up. A few possibilities include:
   - *Beauty*
   - *Facts*
   - *Tolerance*
   - *Success*
   - *Service*
   - *Discipline*
   - *Humility*
   - *Happiness*
   - *Family*

- *Generosity*
- *Opinions*

Make your own list below

2. **Reduce your list to just six values.** Which are most important to you? What do those values mean to you? Take your time.
3. **Are you living your life according to these values?** Consider these parts of your life:
   - *Career*
   - *Relationships*
   - *Hobbies*
   - *Family life*
   - *Goals*
   - Do these parts of your life reflect your values? If not, why? How would your mental clutter be affected if you changed your life to reflect your values?

By defining your values, it becomes much easier to make decisions and set appropriate goals. **When your life is in alignment with your values, your level of mental clutter will decrease.** Adjust your life and activities to match your values.

The next step is to create goals that keep your values in mind. Know your desired outcome and create goals to support that outcome. *When your values, goals, and life purpose match, the resulting synergy makes everything easier, and your efforts become more effective.*

> "Don't dwell on what went wrong. Instead, focus on what to do next. Spend your energies on moving forward toward finding the answer."
>
> *- Denis Waitley*

Mindshift Conclusion

Much of your misery is due to mental clutter. You might have a great life by conventional standards. A nice home, good career, happy family, and a lot of great "stuff." *Your mental clutter can be enough to nullify all of those wonderful things.* Luckily, however, your mental clutter is under your control.

Address all the factors that could be contributing to your mental clutter. Pay attention to your environment, the people in your life, and distractions. These are the triggers that create all of that mental static.

Ultimately, your thoughts and mental habits are the biggest culprit. Focused breathing, meditation, and addressing negative thoughts are the most powerful tools in your arsenal. Use everything at your disposal to create the mental peace you deserve.

Mindshift Two
Understanding Fear and How to Break Through

☙

Fears are a part of life. Everyone is afraid of something. Whether it comes from snakes or spiders, at some point in your life, you're going to experience some degree of fear.

Fear is generally a *good* thing. Yes, you read that right! Fear can spur you to quick action, and even save your life, when there is a real danger. While fear typically has a minimal impact on your life, there are times when fear takes over and becomes a detriment.

If fear is negatively affecting your life, fear not! ***You CAN conquer your fears and live a life free from the pain and apprehension that fear has brought you.***

There are many fears you can overcome with a conscious decision to change your mindset. Practicing some fear-reducing techniques, like those found in this book, may be all you need to rid yourself of them.

Other fears are so extreme that they require professional help. These are deemed phobias, and while they are tougher to crack, conquering these deep-rooted fears is not an insurmountable challenge by any means. With some persistence and willpower, you can even overcome phobias.

In this book, the topic of fear will be discussed in depth. We will delve into fear from all angles, including:

- How fear can negatively affect your life
- The nature of fear
- The difference between a fear and a phobia

You'll also find some tips and techniques to help you overcome your fears, as well as discover the positive results that come from facing your fears head on.

It may seem overwhelming at first, but when you face and conquer your fears, there is a plethora of positive effects that this can have on your life.

The most immediate after-effect is that wave of relief and joy that you feel, knowing that you can overcome obstacles. Once you can think of the thing you feared, and *feel* it is not really so scary after all, you will *know* you have conquered it, and it can never take you captive again!

Facing and conquering your fears will also give you a significant boost in confidence. This will enable you to strengthen other areas of your life, such as:

Work

Romance

Parenting

And more!

The Difference Between Fears and Phobias

Phobias are all the rage in medicine right now. There are phobias for all sorts of things that you wouldn't think would warrant a fearful reaction, like a fear of spiders. But if you're scared of it, it still frightens you and can bring you serious consequences, whether it scares others or not.

While fears and phobias are similar, there is a distinct difference:

Fear is defined as a distressing emotion caused by impending danger or pain; the feeling or condition of being afraid.

A Phobia is a persistent and irrational fear of a specific object, activity, or situation that leads to a compelling desire to avoid it.

In most cases, a phobia causes a detrimental effect in the lives of the people it afflicts. For example, people with agoraphobia, who are afraid of public, open spaces, can end up living their whole lives as shut-ins.

The psychological field has gotten so broad that there are phobias for all sorts of fears, such as:

Mysophobia – Fear of germs

Entomophobia – Fear of bugs

Triskaidekaphobia – Fear of the number 13

Coulrophobia – Fear of clowns

Anthophobia – Fear of flowers

And the list goes on. With some of these fears, feeling some apprehension is perfectly normal. We all want to avoid getting sick, and we may feel nervous when a bee or wasp comes buzzing our way, but the trick is to maintain control and not allow the fear to *rule* you.

While some of these phobias might appear to be silly at face value, they are serious conditions that should be treated as such. If you've been diagnosed with a phobia, you too can overcome it; it just may require professional treatment.

Most likely, as in the vast majority of cases, you experience a simple fear, which can be overcome with a few easy techniques and a healthy dose of willpower.

Is Fear the Mind Killer?

Science fiction fans, cult movie fans, or anyone who's seen David Lynch's 1984 film adaptation of *Dune* may be asking whether or not fear truly is the mind killer, as the film states.

The answer, surprisingly enough, is yes.

Fear has a tendency to overpower rational thought and replace it with sheer panic. Panic is a powerful sensation that can lead to undesired results. This is why you are prohibited from yelling "Fire!" in a crowded movie theater.

In this sense, it *is* something of a mind killer, as you lose yourself in the fear. Like fear, panic is also something that you can overcome.

In a fearful situation, it's important to keep these tips in mind:

1. Stay calm. This is one of the keys to keeping your fear and panic at bay. It may sound like a simple platitude akin to telling a heartbroken friend to get over it, but it really is the best way to face your fears. ***In many cases, you can remain calm by simply avoiding thoughts about your fear.*** For example, if you're afraid of heights and you're about to partake in a ropes course, the only way you're going to get through it is by *not* freaking out about how high up you are. In such a case, the best

way to stay calm is to simply *avoid looking down.* **Focus on your actions** as you tackle the course.

2. Keep your wits about you. Many times, all it takes to get past your fear in a particular situation is to ***focus on a solution*** and take action to implement it.

For example, if you accidentally wander into the vicinity of a beehive or get lost while hiking, you should remain cautious, but keep a cool head. Remember that the bees will not attack you unless provoked, and finding your way back to a main road is usually a simple matter of retracing your steps.

In more perilous situations, the same tips apply. It may sound simplistic, but it's true. For many of these situations, the solutions have been ingrained in your memory; the trick is just to remember them at the appropriate time. Consciously quieting your panic can help you recall critical information.

"*Stop, drop, and roll*" sounds simple enough, but when you actually catch on fire, you may not be thinking about that and will panic. Of course, anyone would, but you can solve the situation much quicker by focusing on what you *can* do to overcome the situation.

Knowledge is Power

It is often said that people fear what they do not understand. As such, a natural way to fight fear is with knowledge.

Horror movies often use this to their advantage, leaving certain things *off* the screen to allow your imagination to do the work for you. ***The directors know that what you don't see is ultimately going to be scarier than something you do see.***

You can use knowledge to combat fear in situations such as these:

1. Monsters under the bed. Surely your kids have encountered that age-old fear of a monster living in the closet or hiding under the bed. In almost every instance, the parental response is to turn on the lights and run an "inspection."

    A good tip in these instances is to let the child see for themself that there's nothing there. While just peeking in the door may work for the night, *showing* the child will surpass telling them that there are no monsters lurking in the bedroom.

2. Medical procedures. The doctor's office can be a nerve-wracking place. This is especially true when major procedures are about to take place. In these situations, doctors will usually take time to explain to their patients exactly what's going to happen. When your doctor gives you this knowledge of the details, it can go a long way toward alleviating your fear. If he doesn't volunteer the information, then ask!

For many fears, a little research to increase your knowledge may enable you to overcome it. ***By knowing your fear, you can remain in control of the emotion and prevent it from overwhelming you.***

You can utilize this tactic in many other situations as well. When fear gets a grip on you, it can sometimes cause your imagination to run wild. By filling your brain with facts, it becomes harder for your mind to conjure up doomsday scenarios to send you into a panic.

All of a sudden, those things that were scary turn out to be quite the opposite. For example, the lurking shadow on the wall is really just a hat rack!

Fear is an Emotion

Show me a person who has never once experienced fear, and I will show you someone with a severe case of denial! ***While it may seem like a weakness in the human condition, fear is a very natural thing.*** Much like happiness or sadness, fear is an emotion.

The trick is to keep that emotion in check. You're going to be afraid of something at some point, and ***how you respond to the fear is more important than the fact that you experienced it.***

Example 1:

Let's say you go out camping with a group of friends for the weekend, and your campsite is approached by a grizzly bear. You're going to be afraid. It doesn't matter how macho you are, if you're approached by a bear, you're going to get scared.

In this case, confronting your fear does not mean literally confronting the bear. However, it's still important that you keep a level head and prevent your fear from taking control.

If you were to panic, start screaming, and run away, this would only result in the bear chasing you, and that bear can run faster than you can.

On the other hand, if you calmly and quietly stand still, you may be able to avoid the bear altogether.

Example 2:

Your friends want to go skydiving. You agree, as everyone who's done it raves about how fun it is. You get on the plane and all too soon the guy looks at you and says, *"You're up."* You look out the hatch and suddenly the idea isn't so appealing. ***This is a perfectly natural response.***

Will everyone feel that sense of dread as they notice how much space lies between them and the ground? Well, there are those who thrive in such situations, but a vast majority of people are going to have second thoughts once they look down.

It's important to keep panic at bay. Whether you decide to jump or not, everything will go more successfully if you can avoid panic and allow clarity of thought.

Since it is an emotion, keeping your fear under control isn't too different from keeping your anger or happiness under control. It's going to be a factor one way or another, but as long as you control it, as opposed to the other way around, you'll be fine. ***Each and every one of us feels fear from time to time. It's what you do with it that's important.***

The High Price of Fear

Fear is a force in and of itself. While it may not seem like it takes that big a toll on your day-to-day life, it can start to add up. The good news is that there's another side to this dilemma.

By conquering your fears, you open up all sorts of doors! You can:

1. Gain confidence. By casting your fears aside, you become a stronger person. Those things that once stood in your way can no longer impede you as you reach new personal heights.

2. Enjoy an increased sense of pride. While conquering your fears will result in more general confidence, you'll also be rewarded with a sense of accomplishment at your ability to master that which has thwarted you for so long.

3. Experience exciting new opportunities. Once you conquer your fears, you'll become open to new experiences that you could not see before because your fears blinded you to the possibilities. With new experiences, you can live a richer life and become the envy of others around you, who wish they could do what you have done.

Each of these benefits enables you to enjoy an endless amount of freedom that has the potential to change your life forever. *You may even find that the thing you once feared is now one of your favorite activities!*

A good example of such a circumstance is with roller coasters. They're fast, they jerk around, and they even have you shooting in a loop. You look at it and think there's no way you're going to get on one.

Maybe it's only because your friends and family bug you about it, but somehow, someway, you make your way onto one. There's a sense of dread as you rise up the first hill, the repetitive clicking of the chains making your heart race even faster.

As you peer over the drop, you may feel a sense of doom, but once the coaster starts bolting and the adrenaline kicks in, it becomes one of the most incredible things you could ever experience.

You, a person who was once wary and fearful of such a pastime, are now clamoring to go on again in order to feel the same rush!

How to Control My Fear?

Practice these strategies to help you conquer your fears:

1. Take a deep breath. This is probably one of the easiest ways to alleviate the sense of dread that accompanies a frightful moment. ***Taking a deep breath slows down your heart rate***

and often delivers a Zen-like calm. *You* can use this technique at any time, making it extremely versatile. No matter what you're encountering, taking in oxygen can always help clear your mind and help you get past whatever fearsome obstacle is impeding you.

2. Hesitation can be a detriment. More often than not, it pays to take a moment to think before doing something drastic. In some situations, however, hesitating can put you at a disadvantage and even allow your fear to turn into panic.

   Take the aforementioned skydiving situation as an example. In this case, hesitation could actually work against you. The more you think about the idea that you're jumping out of a flying airplane, the more afraid you become.

   While it doesn't apply to all situations, there are circumstances where being impulsive can actually be to your benefit. In such situations where immediate action is required, go ahead and just rush in. ***Focusing on your actions takes your mind off your fear.***

3. Remember your training. Throughout your life, you've been trained for many fear-inducing situations, such as fires, tornadoes, and perhaps even using life-saving techniques like CPR. Every time you get on an airplane, they show you what to do in an emergency. ***Be confident that you have the capability to get through these crises when they arise.*** Then let go of the fear!

4. Know your enemy. As previously mentioned, knowledge can ease your fears. By knowing more about the thing that scares you, you automatically reduce the amount of fear because you know the nature of the metaphorical beast. ***Research what you fear and you may find just the thing that conquers the fear itself.***

Fear is a part of everyday life, but that does not mean you have to be a slave to it. On the contrary, you can overcome it and reap all sorts of benefits. You can open yourself up to whole new experiences and possibilities. There is no shame in feeling fear, and some will take longer to overcome it than others, but make no mistake, ***every fear is conquerable.*** With a healthy dose of willpower, you *can* conquer your fears and live a richer, more exciting, and more rewarding life.

Another definition of fear is defined as a biological response to an internal or external stimulus.

- **A biological response.** When you're afraid, your body goes into "fight or flight" mode. Your heart rate goes up, and your adrenaline increases.
- **To an internal or external stimulus.** Fear can arise from within or without. For example, a person thinking about losing their home (internal stimulus) causes fear. Or, a person coming face-to-face with a gun to your head (external stimulus) also causes fear.

All of us struggle with fear and worry from time to time. In fact, in many cases, as stated before, fear is a good and healthy thing. It causes us to wear seatbelts, have safe sex practices, and eat healthier. It's also natural to be concerned about our health, bank account, career status, children, and more.

For example, during the beginning of the COVID-19 shutdown in 2020, many people observed stay-at-home orders. When they were in the community, people practiced socially distancing, mask-wearing, and disinfecting surfaces and hands. But if fear gets out of control, it can take over and prevent us from enjoying life!

When consumed by fear, we cannot be present for others or do the things we love. It also keeps us from taking any risks. We won't start new businesses, write books, or initiate relationships if we're afraid. I was too scared to have authentic relationships in my younger adult years, let alone form them. I always used the excuses of "I don't know what to say," "I'm not good enough," or "I don't have enough money," to avoid doing something that scared me. Eventually, I got tired of singing the "should've, could've, would've," blues. I had no choice but to tap into my courage and break through this fear of relationships. I realized that due to past relationships that ended on a sour note, or past relationships with people who passed away unexpectedly, I had this fear that any connections I would have in the future would inevitably end in heart-shattering disappointment. There was no "happily ever after," so why put in the work, when it would never really pay off? From this moment on, as I continued to put conquering my fear into practice, I began to learn to accept the circumstances I could and could not control. I started to enjoy my journey of self-mastery, or human revolution. Throughout the process of overcoming my deep-seated fear of building and maintaining relationships, I learned, interestingly enough, that my most significant strength is networking and relationship building! If I had not broken through this fear, I would have never recognized one of my biggest strengths, which would have resulted in me not having a relationship with the person who encouraged me to write this book.

If we're going to successfully navigate the often-difficult world in which we live, we need effective strategies for coping with worry and fear.

In my experience, I've learned that most of my fears come from not having or knowing any strategies to deal with my fear. Not dealing with my fear brought worries. **Fear + Worries = Doubt**. I've witnessed this pattern play out too often in my community growing up, and even now. We must ask how we can overcome our fears to move toward what we love and desire.

Let me give you another example. I felt it was time to learn more about the music business. In my heart, I believed I outgrew my circumstances and could no longer emerge living in Milwaukee. I decided to attend the Musicians Institute College of Contemporary Music in Hollywood, California. Two months after I was accepted into the college, I was preparing to leave Wisconsin and attend my courses in the upcoming month. This big fear and worry came over me. I picked up the phone and called the admissions line, "I changed my mind. I will not be attending." The admissions counselor asked, what was the reason for changing my mind? I felt I was not ready. I was worried about not having a place to live and not having enough money. The admissions counselor compassionately shared, "This is a common fear that potential students from out of town have. Often they get discouraged and decide not to attend school. I encourage you to come, but we have enrollment for the following year in January, if you're not ready to come now. I will also send you a list of places you can potentially live here." I told him I would think about it.

Meanwhile, less than two weeks later I was offered a job working third shift as a caregiver at an Adult Family Home. I saved up all the money I earned from the new job and left Milwaukee to attend Musicians Institute in Hollywood. I took the risk on a leap of faith. One of my instructors ended up being Don Grierson, a former A&R executive full of knowledge and experience in the music industry. Don often used the word "risk." Once I graduated from Musicians Institute, Don encouraged me to keep in touch. In fact, Don later became my mentor.

One day while out for dinner with Don, I shared how I almost did not attend Musicians Institute due to my fear and worry. Don shared when he was young and living in Australia, he was at one point working as a disc jockey. After working several years at the radio station, his intuition told him it was time for a new journey. He said he did not know what that specific journey was, but Don believed it was pursuing music in America, a place he had never been before. Don quit his job and booked a reservation on a ship to move to America. Don told me he later canceled the trip because he felt he was not ready, due to fear. He asked for his old job at the radio station in Australia back, even though he knew he still needed to leave. Don later resigned from his position, again, and rebooked another ticket to sail to America. This time around he broke through his fear and actually got on the boat to come to America. Don took the risk. While he was on the ship, he experienced two and a half weeks of nonstop fear. Don then landed in Long Beach, California, where his networking began.

Suppose Don had let his fear drive him. He would not have become one of the best music promoters and music executives in the music industry, and the artists he helped and believed in may not have found the kind of success they have in the music industry. If I had let my fear drive me and not taken the risk to move to Hollywood and attend Musicians Institute, I would not have met Don and not be as knowledgeable and successful as I am today.

George Harrison of the Beatles presenting Don Grierson of Capitol Records the Golden Apple Award for Best Music Promoter.

Tina Turner and Don Grierson, as A&R music executive of CBS Records (Sony), presenting an award for Tina Turner's *Private Dancer* album.

Me and my mentor, legendary Don Grierson, on the set of my music video shoot *Faith Over Fear*

It All Begins with the Music by Don Grierson & Dan Kimpel

EMERGE TO GREATNESS | Haynie Smith | 49

My feature as *Billboard* magazine's R&B/ Hip Hop Power Player.

What you'll probably discover is that most of your fears are internally created.

We are afraid because of what we think will happen rather than what is happening. We feel it's real, but the circumstances we are imagining are not.

I would like to continue with my previous example about moving to California. After seeing the admissions pitch DVD, the co-member of my hip-hop music group Generations Field was the first to decide we should attend Musicians Institute together. As I prepared for us to move, he had a sudden fear and worry. I tried to encourage him to break through the fear, but he let his fear and worry win over him. He did not take the risk.

Almost every day when I attended Musicians Institute in Los Angeles, he called me. He wished he had broken through his fear and decided to participate in college with me. Suppose he had come with me to live in California and attended the Musicians Institute. Who knows what opportunities could have happened for him.

When you understand the true nature of fear, it becomes easier to overcome.

I want you to closely examine your fear and determine if there is any substance to it. When I analyzed why I was so afraid to initiate relationships, I learned the anxiety came from previous personal rejections, thinking I was not ready or just not good enough. With these self-questions, you'll discover proven strategies for facing and overcoming your fears. Are you ready to break through?

Fear Analysis Questions

The following questions are designed to help you analyze your fears. They will help you identify what you are afraid of, see the consequences of your fear, and then take meaningful steps toward overcoming it. When you feel fear start to rise within you, use these 20 questions, write down your answers to get to the root of it, and defeat it.

1. What exactly am I afraid of?

2. Why am I afraid of it?

3. What negative outcomes am I imagining?

4. What thoughts am I trying to avoid?

5. When do I feel most afraid?

6. What things trigger my fear?

7. How is this fear hurting my relationships?

8. How is it keeping me from being happy?

9. How is it hindering me from achieving my goals?

10. How is it taking me out of the present?

11. How is it affecting my health?

12. What opportunities will I miss out on if I give into my fear?

13. How would it change my life if I wasn't afraid?

14. Which elements of this fear are NOT under my control?

15. Am I wasting time and energy on things I cannot control?

16. Which things are under my control?

17. What actions will I take to reduce the *biological* symptoms of fear (exercise, breathing)?

18. How can I replace fear with gratitude?

19. What steps will I take to be mindful and present?

20. Who can I enlist to help me overcome my fears (friend, therapist)?

Change Your Biology

When you're afraid, your body is ramped up, and it can be very difficult to control your thinking. When you dispel the physical effects of fear, it becomes much easier to dispel the mental effects of fear. So, how do you change your biology?

- **Exercise.** When you work out, your body releases endorphins, which make you feel good. If you're feeling worried, go for a brisk walk or hit the gym.
- **Do breathing exercises.** When you're anxious, you breathe rapidly, which raises your heart rate, increases muscle tension, causes dizziness, and more. Focus on changing your breathing patterns.
- **Relax your muscles.** Use progressive muscle relaxation (PMR), a technique for releasing muscles that have been tensed due to anxiety.
- **Eat and sleep right.** As much as possible, try to eat healthy foods and avoid processed ones. Shoot for somewhere between seven to eight hours of sleep each night.

Identify Your Fears

Before you can overcome fear, you must be able to identify it.

If you are not clear regarding the source of your anxiety, you will struggle to resolve it. To identify your fears, ask yourself a series of questions:

1) What am I afraid of?

2) Why am I afraid of it?

3) What do I try not to think about?

4) When do I feel afraid?

5) What emotions do I feel?

6) What negative outcomes am I envisioning?

7) What pictures do I have in my head about this situation?

- **You may need to work a bit to get to the bottom of your fears.** It is common to have smaller fears stacked on top of a much larger one. Work to determine the root fear that is causing all your other anxieties.

- **Next, check each box that applies. Become aware of all the different ways your fear is affecting your life.** Is it:

- Causing you constant emotional distress?

- Keeping you from doing things you want to do?

- Hampering your relationships?

- **The goal of this exercise is to bring you face-to-face with the consequences of your fear.** When you see how worry and anxiety damage your life and hold you back, you become much more motivated to take action.

Practice Worst-Case and Best-Case Thinking

- **When you feel afraid, think about the worst-case scenario.** Now, what are the odds of that *actually* happening? Probably pretty low. The worst case very rarely happens. When you engage in worst-case thinking, you'll often discover that the worst isn't nearly as bad as you think it is.

- **After thinking through the worst-case, think through the best-case.** When you envision the good things that will come your way, it motivates you to take action in the face of your fears. You are able to see what you will miss if you let your worries control you.

Focus on What You Can Control

- **How much time and energy do you spend worrying about things you cannot control?**

A huge portion of life is out of your control, and if you focus on those things, you will be constantly worried. For the most part, you cannot control:

→ The actions and responses of others

→ What others think

→ Aging

→ People's opinions of you

- **Worrying about the things you cannot control is a waste of time.**

When you fear things outside of your control, you have less energy to use on the things where you can make a difference. What can you control?

✓ How you respond

✓ What you think about

✓ The ways you treat others

✓ The information you consume

- **When you focus on what you can control, your fears will significantly lessen, and your life will significantly improve.**

When you find yourself dealing with fear, stop and ask yourself, "*What things are under my control?*" Once you identify those things, give all your time and energy to them.

Choose Gratitude

- **Fear is almost always rooted in a scarcity mentality.** You're afraid that you'll lack:
  - ☹ Love
  - ☹ Respect
  - ☹ Money
  - ☹ Health
  - ☹ Possessions
  - ☹ And more

- **Gratitude completely shifts your perspective, fixing your gaze on the things you already have.** It's hard for gratitude and fear to coexist. When you feel fear beginning to rise in you, embrace gratitude. Look for ways to be grateful that are specifically related to your anxiety.

- **Some simple ways to practice gratitude include:**
  - ☺ Keep a daily gratitude journal.
  - ☺ Send a weekly text message of gratefulness to a friend.
  - ☺ Send out handwritten note cards once a month.
  - ☺ Tell your loved ones why you love them.
  - ☺ Embrace every challenge as an opportunity to grow.
  - ☺ Post about gratefulness on social media.

Practice Mindfulness and Meditation

- **Fear consistently takes you out of the present.** Instead of focusing on the here and now, you are constantly worried about what could happen in the future. Practicing mindfulness and meditation keeps you firmly rooted in the present. All of your energy and focus is given to the current moment.

- **Mindfulness simply means being aware of and savoring the present moment without thought of anything else.** Meditation is a specific practice that helps you grow in mindfulness. Although there are many different forms of meditation, they all involve focusing on the present for a set period of time.

- **If you've never practiced meditation, there are numerous tools available that provide expert guidance:**

    I. **Headspace** has a huge number of guided meditations, sleep sounds, mini-meditations, and more.

    II. **Calm** offers numerous meditations of varying lengths, breathing exercises, nature sounds, sleep stories, and much more.

    III. **Aura** offers personalized meditations, music, stories, and coaching based on your mood.

    IV. **Glo** combines yoga and meditation, allowing you to strengthen your body and mind simultaneously.

Schedule Your Worries

- **One of the big challenges in dealing with fear is that it's always present.** On top of this, many people find it difficult to turn their brains off. Once anxiety has wormed its way into their minds, they can't stop thinking about it.

- **One technique recommended by psychologists is actually scheduling a time when you will think about the things that worry you.**
  - Set aside 15-30 minutes per day.
  - During that time, write down everything that worries you. You don't have to create solutions. You just need to get things down on paper.
  - If you start to worry about something at any other point in the day, tell yourself that you will think about it during your "worry time."
- **In the beginning, you may find it challenging to put off your worries, but over time it will become easier.** An additional benefit of planned worry is that it increases your sense of control over your life.

Get Support

- **Dealing with fear is a lonely battle, often waged just in your mind.** This is why getting support from others is crucial if you regularly deal with worry. When you discuss what you're thinking with others, you'll begin to see your worries from a different perspective.
- **Some ways to get needed support are:**
  - A. **Talk to a friend.** Unburden yourself to someone you know well and can trust.
  - B. **Join an online support group.** There are a number of online organizations specifically designed to help you cope with anxiety.

C. **Join a local support group.** Depending on where you live, there may be in-person anxiety support groups which you can join.

D. **Talk to a Therapist.** There are cultural differences when it comes to deciding therapy.

Finding a therapist to help process your experiences is one of the most important and valuable things you can do for yourself. What is just as important is finding the *right* therapist to do this work with. It took me over a decade to find the right therapist *for me*.

I have had several good therapists before the one I work with now. While I found benefit in working with them, the chemistry to feel genuinely heard and understood was never there. I realized that because there were generational and cultural divides, I couldn't process my experiences with them as thoroughly and meaningfully as I could with my current therapist. I was struggling with working through experiences that were unique to me as a Black man and father. I needed to work with someone who could also understand what it was like to be a Black man and father. The Universe was especially looking out for me when we learned that we were both Hip Hop musicians!

- **Therapists can help you identify what you're afraid of and then guide you forward.** Using both their extensive training and experience, they can give you specific exercises that will help you overcome your fears.
- How do you know if you should go to a therapist? The American Psychological Association poses these questions:
  - *Do you or someone close to you spend some amount of time every week thinking about the problem?*
  - *Is the problem embarrassing, to the point that you want to hide from others?*

- ☐ *Over the past few months, has the problem reduced your quality of life?*
- ☐ *Does the problem take up considerable time (e.g., more than an hour per day)?*
- ☐ *Have you curtailed your work or educational ambitions because of the problem?*
- ☐ *Are you rearranging your lifestyle to accommodate the problem?*

- **When it comes to finding a therapist, you have several options.** You can find one locally. There are also numerous online therapy options available. Most of these online options offer both video sessions and text chat options. They will also try to work with your insurance provider.

- **Do not be embarrassed if you struggle mightily with fear.** Every person has their own share of worries and anxieties. Talking to others about your struggles can go a long way toward helping you make progress.

Have Self-Compassion

- **It is essential to remember that you are not defective if you regularly experience fear and anxiety.** There are many factors that contribute to fear, and you are not choosing to be afraid.

- **In light of this, be compassionate toward yourself.** Avoid trying to deny the existence of your fears or acting like you have it all together. Accept and love yourself, fears and all. If you're unwilling to accept yourself until you completely overcome your fears, you'll be perpetually unhappy.

I Replace Fear With Faith

In these extraordinary times, it is imperative that I pay attention to my emotional state. I realize how easily it is to be triggered at this time. I have learned to let go of those emotions that fail to support me, such as fear, and usher in faith, instead.

I constantly monitor my thoughts and feelings. I take a barometer reading of where I am on the happiness scale. I move the dial up when it gets below neutral.

I choose to unplug from the negative news. I choose to take a break from social media. I let go of people in my life who try to bring me down.

I let go of my addiction to controversial subjects. I let go of the constant bantering of political media. I turn off my television and computer. **I take a break from the external world.**

I choose to spend my time in nature. I like to listen to old-school hip-hop like Mos Def, KRS-ONE, and 2Pac, just to name a few. I find it so peaceful for me to walk in the park or by Lake Michigan. Sometimes I like to drive late at night on the interstate and soak in the serenity of the almost empty highway.

I also read uplifting books. I subscribe to positive publications. I find positive people to have congenial conversations with. I find positive ways of using my time. I use exercise programs that fulfill me. I choose healthy foods. I notice what lifts me up, and I do more of that. I find positive articles that support my faith in life. I recite positive affirmations throughout the day. I feel my mood improving each moment. I make sure I work to stay on the path of transforming fear into faith each day.

Self-Reflection Questions

1. What can I do to strengthen my faith?

2. Whom can I talk with who will help lift me up?

3. How can I be an example of someone who has overcome fear and applies faith principles to their life?

Purchase this pink Faith over Fear t-shirt at https://www.haynie.info/shop or scan the QR Code below.

Purchase this blue Faith over Fear t-shirt at
https://www.haynie.info/shop or scan the QR Code below.

Purchase this black Faith over Fear t-shirt at
https://www.haynie.info/shop or scan the QR Code below.

Scan the QR Code below to download the *Faith over Fear* song for **FREE**, or visit https://www.haynie.info/shop to download the song. After adding song to cart, select "view cart" and enter the promo code No Fear, then proceed to checkout.

Mindshift Three
Be Mindful of Your Thoughts, Make Changes if Necessary

ఴ

If you've ever been frustrated or disappointed in your own thoughts, this will help you make some alterations in your thinking. Changing your mind can be a challenge, especially when you're in trying situations.

Because you are human, you will experience struggles from time to time. But when you commit to applying these healthy strategies, you'll discover success comes with controlling what you think. Each section illustrates situations in which you can benefit, simply by changing your mind.

When You Feel Afraid

Fear is one of the strongest emotions you'll ever feel. ***When you experience fear, your body can go into a state where you either want to fight someone or something, or run away from what's triggering your fear.*** This "fight or flight" syndrome is a normal response, which happens automatically when your body's autonomic system takes over during a crisis.

Yet, there might be other times when you feel fear and then experience frustration with yourself for feeling it. You might notice others around you don't appear to be afraid, and you're a bit vexed about your own emotions. In essence, your emotions may generate fear even when the source of that fear isn't generating fear in others.

For example, you're on a walk with three other friends. Night is starting to fall, and you still have a half-mile to go in order to get back to your house. You feel a bit anxious about getting "caught" out after dark, but you're unsure about why you feel this way.

When you feel fear in situations, but believe it's unwarranted, take these steps:

1. **Confront your fear.** Identify that you're feeling fearful. Label it.
2. **Ask questions.** Ask yourself, "Why am I feeling this way? What is the source of these feelings?"
3. **Examine your past.** Perhaps you've had a prior experience where something scary happened to you when you were in a situation similar to the one you're in now. If there's something traumatizing in your past and it's causing you to feel an overabundance of fear in certain situations, you might want to talk to a professional therapist to see if you can get help in alleviating your unwarranted fears.
4. **Be realistic.** When you're in the situation, ***do you really seem to be in imminent danger?*** A good clue might be looking at those around you to further assess the situation. If others appear relaxed and seem to be having a good time, consider the possibility that your fear is misplaced in this instance.
5. **Share your fears.** When you're open about your fears, it truly helps to dissolve them. Tell your friends when you're feeling

fearful. They'll likely reach out to comfort you through a tough situation.

6. **Learn to soothe yourself.** *It helps if you realize that you're in the best position to calm your own thoughts.* Tell yourself you've made it through many things, and you'll likely make it through the current situation unscathed. If you come to the conclusion there's no real reason to feel afraid, tell yourself it will be okay.

Although you are entitled to your feelings, take the time to explore the reasons for your troubling emotions. Once you determine your feelings may not have a real, believable source, you will be in a better position to conquer them by controlling your thoughts.

> *"It is the mark of an educated mind to be able to entertain a thought without accepting it."*
>
> *- Aristotle*

When You're Consumed with Negativity

Some of us, even though we may not know why, are often focused on the negative aspects of life. ***Do you notice more of the not-so-good elements of your existence rather than focus on the great things happening around you?***

Or you might find yourself being negative in certain situations, like only when you're with your brother or your spouse's family. Consider the situation that's triggering your negativity. If you're consumed with it, then you're not noticing the positivity and brightness around you.

Apply these tips when you recognize you're thinking negatively:

1. **Stay in tune with yourself.** Are you often disagreeing with others or bringing others down by your negative comments? Watch what you're saying to others. Reflect on the reason you might want to bring this negativity.

2. **Ask yourself, "Why?"** What are the reasons you are being negative in the situation? Are you actually a bit envious of your brother because he's doing so well financially? Maybe you didn't really feel like visiting your in-laws, so you're directing your negative feelings toward your partner at the moment. When you figure out whether your negativity is situation-related or maybe because you're just not feeling well this day, you're in a better position to take some steps to control it.

3. **Tell yourself to stop the negativity now.** Although it sounds overly simple, *you're the only one who can truly decide to stop these thoughts.* If it will help, visualize a red octagonal stop sign in your mind's eye. Focus on the stop sign to arrest those negative thoughts.

4. **Recognize.** Rarely does anything positive come from your negativity. Plus, those thoughts tend to make you feel worse about whatever situation you're in.

    - *When you can say to yourself, "My attitude is not helping anything," it shows you recognize the impact of your negativity on yourself and others.*

5. **Challenge yourself.** When you're in a situation that typically triggers your negativity, focus on finding the positives. You may be surprised at what you discover. For example, if you have only tepid feelings about spending time with your in-laws, decide to

discover something positive about them next time. Maybe you share a love for the same type of music, or your mother-in-law loves Will Smith movies just like you do. When you challenge yourself to find the silver lining in a situation, your negativity will dissipate.

Only you have the power to flip your world from darkness to brightness. **Simply by refusing to take the route of negativity, you'll discover the magic of your personal strength.** When you leave the negative behind, you'll discover nothing but positive waiting for you. That's when you know you've taken control of your thoughts in the strongest sense.

> *"Your living is determined not so much by what life brings to you as by the attitude you bring to life; not so much by what happens to you as by the way your mind looks at what happens."*
>
> *- Khalil Gibran*

Deal Quickly with Your Negative Thoughts

Are you plagued by mental negativity? Do you say negative things to yourself? Do you worry about the future? Do you criticize yourself and spend too much time focused on what you lack? That's natural.

Scientists have a theory to explain all this negative thinking.

It was imperative to human survival. Now, it's not helpful anymore.

There was a time that food was scarce. A member of another tribe might beat you to death with a club just for looking at his mate. There were dangerous animals. Those who were overly cautious and worried survived more often than those with a more relaxed attitude.

Your negative thinking is something you inherited. However, it no longer serves you.

Overcome Negative Thoughts

1. **Understand that your negative thoughts are hurting you.** 99% percent of your worries and negative self-talk are harming you. Believe this simple fact, and you're halfway to freedom.

2. **Be observant.** Your new meditation skills will be helpful. Notice when you're having a negative thought.

3. **Distance yourself from the thought.** When you think to yourself, "I'm not good enough to do this," change it to, "I'm having a thought that I'm not good enough to do this."

    - *This simple process puts space between you and the thought.* You realize that it's something separate from you.

4. **Replace the thought.** Reverse the thought. Tell yourself that you're good enough. Tell yourself that things will be okay. Is it true? Well, it's no more of a lie than telling yourself something negative. At least you'll feel better and be in a better position to thrive. Considering that things usually work out, it is more accurate than your negative thoughts.

When You Lack Confidence

Although it would be a lot to ask of yourself to be confident in every situation, it's important to feel as self-assured as possible, regardless of whatever is going on around you. Maybe you occasionally notice you lack feelings of confidence in specific types of situations, like when you're in a group of co-workers, or when you're with someone you see as having the perfect life.

Regardless of what's taking place at the time, control your feelings of low confidence by:

1. **Identifying with your strengths.** *It's good to acknowledge your strengths so you can rely on them when you need some extra confidence.*

2. **Realizing the unique differences among people.** One of your friends might have an expensive car and a great job, and you may envy him for those reasons. But, why not change your focus? You have a spouse whom you love, three kids who adore you, and a comfortable home that brings you hours of pleasure and replenishment.

   - Although your existence is quite different from your friend's, you still have your own set of benefits. Even though you see the great things about the lives of others, you still possess the ability to acknowledge your own treasures.

   - You can feel confident for completely different reasons than your friends do. Their lives have their own special elements, as does yours.

3. **Use journaling.** *Get to the root of what's blocking your confidence by writing about your thoughts.* Include what happened in your day, what you thought, how you felt, and the behaviors you displayed.

   - Seek self-understanding in your writings. Learn as much about yourself as possible.

4. **Consistently move forward, even if it's a little at a time.** The times you're lacking in confidence may be in conjunction with time periods when you feel your life is stagnant.

- When you make this connection, you'll be more likely to keep pushing forward to achieve your goals.
- In the process, you may rediscover your self-assuredness and the will to keep excelling, so you can rise to the top of your game.

You can bolster your own confidence by accepting the fact that your levels of self-assuredness will move up and down over time. However, remain steady on the path of the life you strive for. This ensures your confidence will be consistently there for you.

> *"To enjoy good health, to bring true happiness to one's family, to bring peace to all, one must first discipline and control one's own mind. If a man can control his mind he can find the way to Enlightenment, and all wisdom and virtue will naturally come to him."*
>
> *- Buddha*

When You Wish to Get a Good Night's Sleep

One of the biggest challenges to controlling your thoughts is when you've just laid down to sleep. **Depending on the excitement of the day and the events you've been involved in recently, your thoughts can rob you of a decent night's sleep.**

Put these tips into action to control your thoughts and enjoy a good night's sleep:

1. *Allow your thoughts to flood in.* Initially when you lie down, let your thoughts come into your mind. Give them 5-10 minutes to just do their thing. They'll likely fizzle out during those moments.

2. ***If your mind is pretty active after 10 minutes or so, take control.*** Tell yourself you want to settle down. Acknowledge your day was full or exciting, but now you want to get calm and go to sleep.

3. ***Take four or five deep breaths.*** Breathe air in through your nose and release it through your mouth. When you breathe deeply, it relaxes your body, and you'll be more likely to fall asleep quickly.

4. ***Read a book or listen to the audio version.*** If your body is relaxed or tired enough, you'll notice your eyelids starting to get droopy after you read for a few minutes. As soon as they do, turn off the lights, and don't hesitate to fall asleep quickly.

5. ***Listen to nature sounds or soft calming music.*** I deeply enjoy hearing the sounds of a train horn. This sound places me in a setting of living a simple life in the country where everything is more relaxed and slower. Since I was a child, this sound has appeared to give my mind and body a signal of relief. Another sound that I find helpful is listening to the sounds of nature like rain, gentle wind, cricket, and owls. I also enjoy hearing the songs of Native American flutes.

6. ***Find your comfort temperature for sleep.*** I find it helpful to know what temperature my body likes to relax in. I grew up in the Midwest, where we truly experience the weather of all four seasons. I've learned in the winter, I cannot sleep in a home temperature below 78°. In the summer, I cannot sleep at a temperature above 70°. Practice being mindful of your sleep comfort temperature.

Note: Fighting your thoughts at bedtime can work against falling asleep. Instead, allow in your thoughts, take some deep breaths, and start relaxing to take control of your mind. You have the power to attain the good night's sleep you're after.

> *"Any idea, plan, or purpose may be placed in the mind through repetition of thought."*
>
> *- Napoleon Hill*

When You Want to Be More Productive

Your level of productivity isn't just about how much you work, but also what's going on in your mind. ***The level of productivity you actually achieve is dependent upon how you think.*** In essence, your mind can be your best friend, your worst enemy, or somewhere in between, when you want to put forth your greatest work effort.

If you want to be more productive, put these strategies into play:

1. **Set a specific goal.** In your mind, tell yourself, "I want to make ten sales calls today," or "I will write a list of things to do for tomorrow before the end of today." Establish a productivity goal for yourself.

2. **Avoid feeling overwhelmed.** Instead of allowing those feelings of, "I can't do it," or "This is too much to do," refrain from overthinking. Instead, tell yourself, "This is a lot to do, but I am up for the challenge," or "In due time, I'll get this work done."

    - Changing your thoughts about large projects can make them seem much easier, enabling you to approach them with gusto and get them done.

3. **Acknowledge the progress you've made.** At the end of the day, think about what you achieved. "I started decluttering my house. I am not finished but I can feel the energy of less clutter!" Resolve to focus on what you've accomplished rather than on what you have yet to do.

4. **Block out the negative vibes.** If you dwell on negative thoughts and feelings, you'll only get bogged down. Instead, refuse to let them in and be relentless about charging forward and getting things done.

5. **Practice meditation.** Those who meditate on a regular basis experience many benefits: they live calmer lives, have the confidence to make it through the tough spots, and are less affected by overwhelming situations. By simply meditating twice a day for 10-30 minutes, you can gain back your power and give 100% to your work.

Achieving the level of productivity you want is completely up to you. Your mindset and thoughts make all the difference when it comes to accomplishing what you hope to achieve. When you recognize the results you can achieve, it will be easier to make a consistent effort to alter your focus, change your feelings, and become more productive.

"Nobody can change your mind. You must take that responsibility all by yourself."

- Anonymous

When Your Anger is Ruling Your Life

We all feel angry occasionally. Anger is a normal human feeling. However, does your anger seem like it has crept into every corner of your life? Is it taking over?

It may be your family, co-workers, friends, or even yourself that's causing you anger. If this anger is overflowing into other facets of your life, do something about it. *A life filled with anger is a life requiring changes.*

Apply these strategies when you feel angry and wish to change how you feel:

1. **Localize it.** Spend some "alone-time" thinking about who or what is triggering the anger. Are you angry at a situation or a person? Rather than spreading your anger throughout your life, get it focused so you understand exactly why you're angry.

2. **Acknowledge your lack of control over certain situations and people.** When you acknowledge that you're unable to control some events and other people, you can let it go and focus on moving forward with things you *can* control. It's true that you can't control what another person says or does. So sometimes, you just need to remind yourself of this to help you better control your anger.

3. **Tell yourself you have the power.** You're the only one who can make the decision to stop your anger. Will it be easy? Probably not. But a big part of being angry is feeling powerless over a situation.

    - Tell yourself that you have the power to curb your anger. It will make you feel better.

4. **Release it.** It's easier said than done to just "let go" of your anger. But the reality is, if you can begin practicing this technique, *your life will get easier.*
   - For example, if you're mad at your parents for telling you they're leaving $50,000 to their favorite animal charity instead of you, accept the situation and move on with your own life.
   - **Think of things you can do instead of being angry.** Be proud of your parents for caring about animals, be awed by their generosity to others, and follow in their footsteps when it comes to being kind to animals.
5. **Change the scenery.** Remove yourself from a situation or people who are triggering your angry feelings. For example, take a walk, go for a ride, or go work in your yard.
6. **Focus on yourself.** What are your goals? What do you hope to achieve? Put your emotional energy back into your own life where it belongs. Rejuvenate your spirit and move toward achieving your dreams.

There's no room for anger in a life well-lived. When you promise yourself you won't be consumed by the poison of anger, you'll become tranquil and more pleased than you ever thought possible.

"Your heart will try to change your mind, but your mind knows what's best for you."

- Sonya Parker

When Determining If You Should End an Unhealthy Relationship

Although you might think you're stuck in a relationship that brings you down, the fact is, your mind is what's stuck. You keep thinking the same particulars over and over again, and you've convinced yourself that you're unable to change or end the relationship.

The good news is, you can control your thoughts when it comes to trying to figure out how to handle unhealthy relationships. However, it isn't always easy.

To make relationship decisions that serve you well, try this process:

1. **Review the pros of your relationship.** Write down the positive aspects of your relationship. Does your current relationship allow you to enjoy 75% of what you're after in a relationship?

2. **What leads you to believe the relationship is unhealthy?** Also, write down those cons of your relationship. How do your two lists measure up? Are the items on your con list fixable? If you find yourself feeling afraid of your partner or being concerned about your children, these are red flags to break away from that person or at least seek expert guidance.

3. **Look at the bottom line.** What will you lose if you end the relationship? What will you gain if you choose to stay and work things out? Refuse to allow sympathy or concerns for your partner to determine your final decision as to whether you should stay or go. Although they may love you and you may love them, sometimes love isn't enough. If your partner is threatening you or constantly making remarks which are

damaging to your self-esteem, consider the ultimate results of their behavior.

4. **Remind yourself you're only as trapped as your mind allows you to be.** Situations can almost always be changed. Regardless of whether you live in the same home, or are just dating, there is a way out for you. It just depends on whether you choose to pursue it. Never remain in an unhealthy relationship you really want to escape from because of feeling trapped.

   - Some people use a lack of money as an excuse for staying in a contentious relationship. If this factor concerns you, make a financial exit plan that could work for you.

   - Use your mind to "untrap" yourself by changing how you're viewing the situation.

5. **Make an exchange in your thoughts.** You can switch your thinking from, "I'm caught up in this bad relationship," to "I have the power to change this relationship by changing my outlook." Decide to think about creating the positive relationship you want and doing what's necessary to meet this goal, rather than going over and over the negatives of it.

6. **Change your behavior now.** If you're in a troublesome relationship, you can switch how you behave and react. This may allow you to overcome some of the difficulties. If you normally argue back when your spouse raises their voice to you, stop and listen to what they have to say instead. Make a concerted effort to understand your partner.

7. **Find a neutral person to talk to.** It can help immensely to speak to someone who's completely uninvolved with you and your situation. Talking to a friend or family member may also

be helpful, but they are usually too emotionally invested in your life to give unbiased advice. You may want to consider talking to a therapist or counselor who is a neutral party and trained to listen. Sometimes it really helps to hear yourself saying aloud what conditions you've been living in, thinking about, and being part of, in a questionable relationship. Verbalizing this may help compel you to make the best decision for yourself, whether it's staying or getting out of the relationship.

Controlling your thought process when it comes to relationships can be quite a challenge. You may have gotten used to how things have been. Or you may simply feel unsure about what to do next.

After you identify the pros and cons of remaining in a relationship or leaving it, you can then proceed to the next steps to determine what you should do next. By following these strategies, you'll be able to clarify in your mind what is best for you and your specific situation.

"Do not dwell in the past, do not dream of the future, concentrate the mind on the present moment."

- Buddha

When You Want to Feel Comfortable Being Alone

One of the most trying situations for many of us is learning how to be alone. Your mind may interpret spending time alone as, "Nobody wants to be with me," "I must be a loser," or "I feel unsafe when I'm alone."

Yet it's wise for us to get comfortable with solitude, quiet, and aloneness. ***We can find peace and time for our solitary pursuits when*** *we are by ourselves.* There are plenty of reasons to get comfortable with being alone.

If you're struggling to cope with being by yourself, employing these strategies will help:

1. **Acknowledge that alone time is different.** No one else is present for you to watch or listen to. You have no one to talk to in person. Being alone is in a class all by itself.

2. **It's okay to be alone.** Simply tell yourself that everyone's alone from time to time, and there's really nothing unusual about it. *Recognizing and accepting solitude as part of the human condition will help you adjust to the experience.*

3. **Consider being alone as a time to focus on yourself.** Learn to cherish your alone time. It belongs only to you, and you can think or do whatever you like during those times.

    - While you're alone, ask yourself what you hope to achieve within the next six months or year and make exciting plans to move forward toward your dreams.

    - Another great use for time alone is to take advantage of the time to engage in activities that bring you joy. Perhaps you would like to pursue a new hobby or art. You'll reap happiness, serenity, and contentment from your time alone.

    - Whatever you decide, even if you just want to take a nap in your alone time, *you'll feel rejuvenated and ready to face the world when you take time just for you.*

You *can* change your thinking about spending time by yourself. One key to a happier life is learning to take advantage of time you have alone to do as you wish.

> "The need for change bulldozed a road down the center of my mind."
>
> *- Maya Angelou*

Mindshift Conclusion

You set the pace for exercising the power to control your own thinking. **Although you can seek out guidance or assistance from others, you're ultimately the one to make the final choice about changing your thinking.** You're responsible for everything going on in your head.

Step up to take control and change your thoughts from the negative feelings and beliefs that hold you back to positive thoughts that will serve you well for the rest of your life.

> "As a single footstep will not make a path on the earth, so a single thought will not make a pathway in the mind. To make a deep physical path, we walk again and again. To make a deep mental path, we must think over and over the kind of thoughts we wish to dominate our lives."
>
> *- Henry David Thoreau*

Mindshift Four
Believe in You, Practice Self-Reliance!

☙

Self-reliance means different things to different people. The famous author, Ralph Waldo Emerson, considered self-reliance to be the avoidance of conformity and foolish consistency. He believed people should develop their own ideas and beliefs.

To others, self-reliance means stockpiling five years' worth of food, buying a diesel generator, and building a bomb shelter.

From a practical viewpoint, a self-reliant person is able to pursue original thoughts and ideas, while successfully navigating the basics of life without an unreasonable amount of assistance.

This includes the ability to procure food and shelter, live a healthy lifestyle, earn a living, and maintain healthy relationships.

Total self-reliance is neither possible nor desirable. No one can handle the challenges of modern life without the assistance of others. Sooner or later, you'll need legal assistance, a new transmission, or a trip to the emergency room.

Total self-sufficiency would also exclude others from your life. Relationships are an important part of the human experience. Imagine how empty life would be without others to share in life's ups and downs. What's important is learning to take care of yourself to the best of your ability.

> *"It is easy in the world to live after the world's opinion; it is easy in solitude to live after our own; but the great man is he who in the midst of the crowd keeps with perfect sweetness the independence of solitude."*
>
> **- Ralph Waldo Emerson**

Pitfalls of Dependence

The opposite of self-sufficiency is dependence. If you rely excessively on friends, family, romantic partners, drugs, or televisions, you're not being self-reliant. A self-reliant person can deal effectively with boredom, emotions, and other challenges.

An unhealthy dependence on others will sap your belief in yourself. Dependence is the ultimate expression of incompleteness. Do you depend on others to complete you?

We often seek people, things, relationships, activities, and places to fulfill emotional needs. This is not self-sufficiency.

That's not to say that the people, things, and activities in your life can't be appreciated and enjoyed. Rather, if you're self-reliant, your well-being and happiness are not totally dependent upon them.

> *"The trick is in what one emphasizes. We either make ourselves miserable, or we make ourselves happy. The amount of work is the same."*
>
> **- Carlos Castaneda**

Benefits of Self-Reliance

Consider the advantages that self-reliance can bring you:

1. **Maximize self-esteem.** There's nothing more soul crushing than needing help with something that everyone else seems to be able to handle alone. Whether it's paying your bills or getting across town, when you constantly need help, you lose a little bit of your self-esteem each time.

2. **Increase self-confidence.** When you can take care of business effectively, your confidence in yourself grows.

3. **Your successes and failures are your own.** There's no one else to blame. You make your own decisions and take your own course of action. You can enjoy the fruits of your successes and benefit from your mistakes. If you allow someone else to make your decisions for you, you'll never know if your instincts were right or wrong. Maybe you had a better way.

4. **You have everything you need.** *You can manage the world on your own terms.* You have more options available to you than those who are dependent. You can move through the world more easily.

5. **You maximize your ability to grow.** By depending on yourself, you will have more opportunities to grow and develop. You can learn about yourself in a way that others cannot.

6. **You won't be socially dependent.** You cannot be authentic if the opinions of others matter to you. If you are concerned whether your actions are popular, you are at the mercy of others. You are free from this burden if you are self-reliant.

7. **You are a joy to be around.** *Self-sufficiency means that you provide more than you take away.* You provide more support than you take. You contribute more than you consume.

   - Do you have a friend or family member that takes more than they provide? They wear you out, don't they?

Self-reliance is not for the faint of heart, but the benefits are enormous. By building your self-reliance, you will be helping yourself and others. Reach for your best and build your ability to be self-reliant.

> *"If you truly want to be respected by people you love, you must prove to them that you can survive without them."*
>
> *- Michael Bassey Johnson*

5 Pillars of Self-Reliance

- ☺ Good health
- ☺ Individuality
- ☺ Mental toughness
- ☺ Relationships
- ☺ Financial stability

Maximizing each of these areas will provide the greatest opportunity for self-reliance.

Health

Consider implementing these habits to allow your health to support your self-reliance:

1. **Place a priority on daily physical activity.** It's a mistake to believe that one can exercise a few times each week for an hour

and be physically vibrant. It's not necessary to run a five-minute mile, but it is necessary to move your body each day.

- The more you move, the more energy you will develop. ***Having more energy results in an enhanced ability to manage your life.***
- Excessive sitting has become the latest epidemic. Sedentary jobs and lifestyles have become the norm. Get up at least once each hour and talk a short walk.

2. **Visit the doctor.** You might feel perfectly fine, but there are several serious ailments that have few symptoms until your health is in real jeopardy:

- Hypertension
- Diabetes
- Cancer
- Heart disease
- High cholesterol
- Many sexually transmitted diseases
- Osteoporosis
- This is just the short list!

Many of us, particularly men, avoid a yearly visit to the doctor. ***Many serious conditions are treatable and even preventable if caught early.*** Be brave. Visit your physician regularly.

3. **Follow a healthy diet.** It can be confusing to choose an eating style. There are so many options. However, you already know which foods are healthy and which are not. At the very least, drop the unhealthy foods from your diet and add more

fruits and vegetables. Consult with your doctor for additional guidance.

- Avoid underestimating the value of a healthy diet. Most of the diseases listed in the previous point are preventable with a diet that supports good health.
- Your diet also includes beverages. Focus on drinking more water and avoid excessive amounts of caffeine.
- If you want to embrace the ultimate in self-reliance, take up gardening. You can control the quality of your food supply and get more exercise.

4. **Get enough sleep.** Sleep studies show that most of us would benefit from additional sleep. If you are well rested, you will perform better at work and have more energy for your family. You will also boost your health.

5. **Live a healthy lifestyle.** We all face choices each day that either risk or preserve our health. Staying out at a bar until 3am is not healthy. Driving on worn tires is risky. Before making a decision, reflect on how it might impact your life.

Place a priority on your health. ***Everything becomes more challenging when your health is compromised.*** Your health status is most affected by your daily habits. Strive to take good care of yourself each day and visit your physician regularly.

"You cannot help people permanently by doing for them, what they could and should do for themselves."

- Abraham Lincoln

Individuality

The most valuable parts of you are the parts that are unique. Gold and diamonds are valuable because they are rare. Your hands and feet are valuable to you, but the rest of the world doesn't care. There are plenty of hands and feet. Your ability to drive a car or speak English is commonplace. Ask yourself these questions below and write down your answers:

1. What can I do better than the average person?

2. How can I take advantage of that?

3. Can I build a career around my uniqueness?

4. What is my greatest strength?

The advantages of individuality are significant:

1. **You can contribute to the world in a more meaningful way.** You are able to think outside the box and provide new solutions. You have the emotional freedom to share your ideas openly.

2. **Your ability to influence and inspire others is enhanced.** When you are able to take a stand or share a new perspective, others are inspired to do the same. The freedom that you demonstrate to others is uplifting. Show others how to be free and put their own unique stamp on the world.

3. **You are free of the opinions of others.** Imagine making decisions without worrying about what others will think! It is common for people to impose their fears on others. You can be free of that burden. You can think for yourself.

4. **Your self-esteem is higher when you are comfortable being yourself.** How many times have you said to yourself, "I should've _____, but I was afraid of looking like an idiot."?

    - **When we fail to do or say what we know to be "right," our self-esteem takes a beating.** While it can be stressful in the short-term, following one's conscience is satisfying after the smoke has cleared.

A healthy dose of individuality is a component of self-reliance. However, avoid the need to separate yourself from others. Seek yourself rather than avoid the crowd. If you avoid what everyone else is doing, you are still dependent on others.

Showing your individuality is difficult if you have been a conformist throughout your life. There's no need to build your individuality. You already have it. *The key is to allow the world to see it each day.* Practice makes perfect.

Take these steps to nurture your individuality:

1. **Embrace your uniqueness.** Recognize that your unique talents and view of the world are valuable.

2. **Identify your values.** It is important to know your values. While it's important to avoid conforming blindly, it's just as important not to shun all convention without giving the situation some thought.

    - If you are aware of your values, it will be much easier to make wise choices. Sticking to your values also makes it easier to challenge the status quo.

3. **Start small.** *Be brave enough to stand out in some small way.* Maybe it's a crazy pair of socks or a mailbox that looks like a

doghouse. What can you do to show your individuality without giving yourself a panic attack?

4. **Try one new thing you've been too embarrassed to do in the past.** Have you always wanted to learn how to write a rap? Maybe you've always wanted to write a scandalous novel. After a few smaller victories, you'll be ready for something bigger. ***Your self-esteem and enjoyment will soar.***

5. **Learn to ignore those who do not support you.** If you don't want to deal with any naysayers, the only solution is to stay at home. You're going to be criticized no matter what you do and where you go. You may as well do the things you love along the way.

6. **Find others who have an individual streak.** You'll be inspired and feel comfortable around them.

Be yourself. ***Show yourself that you are good enough.*** You're not just helping yourself. You are helping others, too.

> *"We are so accustomed to the comforts of "I cannot," "I do not want to," and "it is too difficult," that we forget to realize when we stop doing things for ourselves and expect others to dance around us, we are not achieving greatness. We have made ourselves weak."*
>
> *- Pandora Poikilos, Excuse Me, My Brains Have Stepped Out*

Mental Toughness

Mental fortitude is invaluable. It will allow you to persevere during challenging circumstances. It will also allow your individuality to grow.

When you hit a financial snag, do you call your parents or find a way out of your mess? Do you become overwhelmed? Or do you get busy and create solutions? Mental toughness is an important part of self-reliance.

Develop your mental toughness with these strategies:

1. **Maintain positive thoughts.** Become aware of your thoughts and the things you say to yourself.

    - Negative thoughts can influence your beliefs and actions. ***Telling yourself, "I can't do anything right," will wear down anyone's confidence after a while.***
    - You cannot reach your full potential if your thoughts are betraying you.
    - Keep your thoughts positive and relevant. It requires a lot of attention to monitor your thinking.

2. **Learn how to deal with discomfort.** All animals avoid discomfort. It's part of our DNA. However, you can build tolerance to discomfort, just as you can build tolerance to exercise.

    - **Learn to accept what you are feeling.** You might be anxious, angry, or scared, but you are not required to be influenced by these feelings. Recognize your feelings and allow them to exist. Remember that you are in control.
    - **Avoid being impulsive.** Suppose you're working on an important task at work and you have the urge to quit. Stick with it for another 15 minutes before switching tasks. When you have the urge to eat a snack, force yourself to wait. Rather than giving in to your impulses, put them off. Your ability to wait and persevere will grow with practice.
    - **Breathe.** When you start to feel uncomfortable, take a few deep breaths and relax.

3. **Stay focused.** Keep your attention on the task. If your mind is focused, you'll have an easier time keeping any negative emotions at bay.

4. **Take cold showers.** Not only will cold showers increase your mental toughness, the activity has been shown to boost the immune system. *You will be amazed at how your ability to deal with discomfort strengthens with time and practice.*

5. **Be a finisher.** Too many people give up near the end. Avoid leaving the greasy roast pan in the sink until tomorrow. Trim the lawn after you've finished mowing. Avoid leaving tasks 90% completed. Practice getting things done.

6. **Meditate.** It's easy to quit when you look at the future and think about how long something is likely to take. Meditation will teach you how to be present, instead, and help you persevere.

Building your mental toughness takes time and effort. It's no different than building your ability to exercise. As your strength and experience grow, you will be able to deal with larger challenges. *Focus on small advances in your mental toughness.* Be proud of your progress. As your ability to handle difficult challenges increases, your self-sufficiency will increase as well.

> *"Sure, it sucked to be lost, but I'd long ago realized I preferred it to depending on anyone else to get me where I needed to go. That was the thing about being alone, in theory or in principle. Whatever happened - good, bad, or anywhere in between - it was always, if nothing else, all your own."*
>
> *- **Sarah Dessen, Lock and Key***

Make room into your day to recharge.

When life throws me for a loop, I step back and give myself time to recover. Renewal is a formidable source of positive energy. I listen to cues from my body to know when to take a break. When aloofness starts to set in, I know that it is time to focus on other things. **Balance is important to my overall success in life.** Making time for that balance is one way for me to recharge. I switch between work and social interaction when I feel my energy waning.

Spending time alone without thinking about work or the worries of the world gives me an intense jolt of positivity. My special alone activity serves as the boost that pushes me toward challenging goals. Recharging means focusing on things that stimulate my mood. Reading books, traveling by car, and being still in a quiet place or town all give me a feeling of blissful satisfaction. Whenever I start to feel jaded, I know that it is time for me to do something that sparks joy. Say this affirmation below three times during your daily recharge and after. Your energy will recharge!

Today, I am committed to keeping myself charged up so that I am always conscious of the beauty of life. My happiness depends on my ability to step back from the hustle and bustle and choose simple pleasures that renew me.

Self-Reflection Questions: Write your answers.

1. What are some of my favorite alone time activities?

2. How do I go about scheduling downtime into my hectic workdays?

3. How does my body feel when it is time to recharge?

Relationships

Relationships are a tricky area. It is easy to become dependent on others. Some of the people in our lives are so willing to help that they actually encourage us to be anything other than self-reliant. Having the right mix of people in your life will enhance your ability to depend on yourself. It is difficult to thrive without sharing experiences with others. Feelings of loneliness will hamper your ability to take care of yourself.

Consider these ideas for developing healthy relationships that also support your self-reliance:

1. **Build empowering relationships.** There are plenty of self-reliant people out there. Include a few of them in your life.

    - Find people that will encourage and support you. Find people that inspire you.
    - Healthy relationships actually enhance your ability to be self-reliant.

2. **Avoid dependency.** It's easy to rely on others when we are feeling lazy or incapable. Everyone has a tough day now and then. We all need to rely on others from time to time, but avoid unhealthy dependence.

3. **Give more than you receive.** This is perhaps the best way to ensure the relationship is not creating dependence. On the other hand, be careful that the relationship is not costing you too much either. *Your self-sufficiency is decreased when others take too much from you.*

4. **Be able to walk away.** Be able to let go of unhealthy relationships. There are other fish in the sea.

A full life requires the presence of others. ***Build and maintain healthy relationships, and your self-sufficiency will be enhanced.*** Poor relationships sap your resources and can create dependency.

> *"It is folly for a man to pray to the gods for that which he has the power to obtain by himself."*
>
> *- Epicurus*

Financial Stability

It's much easier to care for yourself if you have the financial means to do so. Even a middle-class lifestyle isn't cheap. Regardless of your income, living below your means is necessary to deal with the inevitable financial hiccups. If your finances are shaky, your ability to be self-reliant is hampered.

Increase your financial stability to increase your self-reliance:

1. **Have a sufficient source of income.** A safe and healthy existence isn't free. To have true self-sufficiency, it is important to have a sufficient income. ***Seek ways to increase your income if you're not earning enough.***

2. **Have a stable source of income.** The stability of your income is also important. If your income varies significantly from week to week, make an effort to find some stability.

   - A second source of income can greatly enhance your financial stability. If you lose one source, you'll still have money coming in.

3. **Save regularly.** Few of us have an income that can weather any storm. It is necessary to save in case of an emergency.

- Financial experts recommend an emergency fund of three to six months of living expenses. Even after you have achieved this milestone, continue saving. Be prepared for any financial disaster.
- Prepare for retirement. If you want to be self-reliant, save enough money to fund your retirement.

4. **Live modestly.** You are not self-reliant if your life revolves around debt. ***Debt only decreases your ability to care for yourself in the long term.*** Avoid the belief that consumption is the key to happiness. **Being debt-free is the ultimate freedom.**

- A modest lifestyle will also increase the amount you are able to save.

Build your financial resources and your ability to handle financial challenges. Money is an important resource, and true independence is much more challenging without it. **Avoid being at the mercy of financial emergencies.**

> *"Associate with the noblest people you can find; read the best books; live with the mighty. But learn to be happy alone. Rely upon your own energies, and so not wait for, or depend on other people."*
>
> *- Thomas Davidson*

Mindshift Conclusion

It is not necessary to grow your own food or build your house by hand. Leave the excessive food storage practices to the preppers of the world. ***Healthy self-reliance involves building your internal and external resources to provide you with more freedom and control over your life.***

With sufficient financial resources, it is not necessary to spend a lot of time worrying about the external resources. Focus on your inner resources.

Take care of your health. Nothing will degrade your ability to be self-sufficient more than failing health. Exercise, eat, sleep, and visit the doctor. Make healthy choices.

Allow your individuality to grow and shine. ***It is your greatest resource.*** Learn to make decisions for yourself. Feel free to seek expert advice, but take responsibility for making the final decision. Grow your self-esteem and confidence. ***Learn from your mistakes***.

Enhance your mental toughness. The more you can handle yourself, the less dependent you will be on others. You'll have the ability to persevere and finish what you've started.

Relationships make the world go round and add value to life. However, it is important to avoid becoming so dependent on your relationships that you inhibit your individuality and self-reliance. Add more to your relationships than you take. Be prepared to move on if a relationship is not adding value to your life.

Self-reliance is not shutting yourself off from the world. ***Self-reliance is building yourself up to your potential.*** Take responsibility for your words and actions, and you will find that you have greater control of both your present and your future.

Mindshift Five
Rebuild Your Self-Esteem

☙

"You yourself, as much as anybody in the entire universe, deserve your love and affection."

- Buddha

Have you ever wished that you felt better about yourself? Maybe you've felt kind of "blah" about your life and where it's going. The good news is, if you put your mind to it, you do have the power to grow your self-esteem! **When you do, you'll also, as a happy result, turn up your passion and galvanize your efforts to live the life you seek and deserve.**

This Mindshift provides specific actions to take in seven different areas of your life to achieve greater self-esteem:

- Discover how your job can increase positive feelings about yourself.
- How to use your thoughts to feel better about yourself

- The importance of doing some physical and emotional "housecleaning"
- Engaging regularly in cherished activities to cultivate feelings of self-love and self-worth
- In reconnecting with your life roles as a partner and parent, you will find your opinion of yourself improves quickly.
- Your physical well-being is intimately aligned with what you think and believe about yourself, so we have included a chapter about how to enhance your physical self.
- Finally, learn the powerful impact that recognizing your uniqueness can have on your efforts to increase your self-esteem.

Begin your journey now to construct self-esteem that will drive you to valiantly create the existence you have always dreamed of for you and your family.

"A man is but the product of his thoughts; what he thinks, he becomes."

- Mahatma Gandhi

Apply Yourself at Work to Increase Your Self-Esteem

One of the main sources of your self-esteem as an adult is your career. **Regardless of the kind of work you do, it is important to recognize its value in your life.**

Your job is the source of your livelihood. It provides much of the main structure to your existence. How you feel about your work plays a major role in how you feel about yourself.

Hopefully, you have a positive view of your career and put forth your best efforts at work. But even if you don't, it's time to realize its impact on your life. Your work can bring you positive experiences, feelings, and self-esteem if you choose to apply yourself.

Consider these points to galvanize your job efforts and pump up your self-esteem:

1. **Discover the value in working hard.** No matter how you feel about your job, if you can reframe it so you focus on your efforts, your self-esteem will improve. Whether you're working diligently at filing and answering the phones or making as many sales calls as you can in a day, you'll feel better about yourself.

   - At the end of the day, when you step back and look around at all you accomplished, you can't help but have positive feelings.

2. **Learn to love your job.** After all, someone somewhere benefits because of the work you complete. Work toward finding an inner peace related to your career.

   - *Make a conscious decision to love your work.* In order to allow yourself to love your job, let go of the negativity and seek to find the love for what you're doing for a living. There is something positive to be said about every job.

   - Identify the positives of your job and focus on them each day. Make something great happen by loving your job.

3. **Be the best** office assistant, garbage collector, or insurance agent you can be. What will it take for you to be the star worker at your workplace? If you're unsure where to start, begin observing a co-worker whom you believe does a top-notch job.

- How does the person conduct himself? What do you notice about their work ethic? What about work habits? Do they consistently arrive early and stay a bit late? Perhaps they ask questions to clarify assignments and work creatively on each project.

- Use your observational skills to find out how to be the best, and then apply what you've learned to rise to the top.

Putting your nose to the grindstone will aid you to rediscover what's important to you in terms of your career. **Make every effort to reconnect with your job.** When you see the value of working hard, decide to love your job, and strive to be the best worker you can, you'll increase your self-esteem tenfold.

> *"Work joyfully and peacefully, knowing that right thoughts and right efforts will inevitably bring about right results."*
>
> **- James Allen**

Use Your Cognitions to Build a Positive View of Yourself

Although self-esteem has to do with how you feel, you can affect your level of self-esteem by using your thoughts or "cognitions." The good news is, you have control over your thoughts and can change them if it will help you feel better or progress toward improved self-esteem.

Survey this list of strategies to utilize your cognitions to increase your self-esteem:

1. **Refrain from negative self-talk.** What do you say when you talk to yourself? Perhaps you say mostly positive things. "I know I'm going to do a good job," or "No one can make better

cookies than I can," are examples of positive self-talk that serve to enhance how you feel about yourself.

- On the other hand, negative self-talk can be destructive to your self-esteem. Examples of negative self-talk are comments like, "I know I'll never amount to anything," or "My boss will never pick me to work on an important project."

- Strive to avoid negative self-talk by practicing the subsequent strategies in this chapter.

2. **Learn to distract yourself from negative thoughts.** As soon as you begin to think negatively, it is your responsibility to change those thoughts.

    - Notice right away when negativity is floating through your mind. Then, make a decision to think about something else.

    - Tell yourself, "I'm not going to think about that right now. Instead, I'm going to watch a movie." Or you could say, "I'm going to do something positive right now, like wash the car."

    - *The key is to be aware of your thoughts so you can immediately change your thinking (and perhaps your activity) at the time you begin thinking negatively.*

3. **Reflect on your successes.** Remembering what you've done well in the past will help you gain some wind beneath your wings. When you remind yourself that you've enjoyed some great successes, you'll realize that you can also have great success in your present and future.

    - Consider the skills and character traits that helped you succeed. Perhaps you used patience and tact when dealing with someone in power over you. Maybe you persevered through a very rough time by thinking positively and received a promotion as a result.

- *Those elements are still inside of you.* Vow to rediscover the aspects of yourself that kept you going to achieve past successes. You'll feel great about yourself.

4. **Do some self-evaluation—what are you really good at?** Delve in further to your personality and preferences. ***List the talents, skills, and activities you do well.***

    - Perhaps you are creative and make beautiful scrapbooks or like to stay busy so everything around the house is always in tip-top condition. Maybe you decided to get in shape a few years ago and have done a great job maintaining your good health.

    - Look deep inside to acknowledge what you excel at. As you recognize the positive traits within you, you'll realize you have a lot of reasons to have a healthy self-esteem.

5. **What positive elements do people notice about you?** Do they say, "You're really good with numbers," or, "You type faster than anyone I know?"

    - ***Recognize that people usually don't make complimentary statements unless they really believe you possess those qualities.*** Use those statements to remind yourself of more positives about yourself. Find personal strength in the idea that you're good at some things and people notice.

It's smart to use your thoughts however you can to feel better about yourself. Avoid engaging in negative self-talk. Distract yourself when you begin to think negatively. Ponder past successes and think about what you're good at. Take a look at what others say you do well. Realign your thoughts to produce more self-esteem and you will like what happens.

> *"Once you replace negative thoughts with positive ones, you'll start having positive results."*
>
> **- Willie Nelson**

Do Some Housecleaning— Physically and Emotionally

When you're looking to ignite your passion, it's helpful to live an uncluttered existence, physically and emotionally. Have you considered that maybe it's time to do a bit of housecleaning?

Whether it's your physical or emotional "environment" that is cluttered, why not gussy up your surroundings?

Ponder these points:

1. **Clutter is a deterrent to positive self-esteem.** Because clutter in and of itself is distracting, it's wise to tidy up the world around you. Physical clutter draws your attention away from what's important and on to the messy situations surrounding you. Emotional clutter serves to do the same thing, to divert attention from what really matters.

    - *Banishing chaos and messy spaces from your life will help you regain the space to work on things that matter to you.* When you do, you'll build your self-esteem immensely.
    - If you're unsure about the suggestion to physically clean up your surroundings, try cleaning out just one drawer,

cabinet, or closet. You'll see you completed a task and made something better. Then, you'll feel pretty good about it.

- If you're overwhelmed at the prospect of getting your home in order, start small. For example, focus on one room at a time, or even one corner of the room, or a piece of furniture that's piled with clothing.

2. **Bring order into your life.** When there's order in your home, you can look around and feel good about your environment and yourself. You'll feel calmer and self-esteem will grow.

    - Elicit your partner's help to get things organized at home.

3. **Examine your close relationships.** Our close relationships have a profound impact on how we feel about ourselves. If you're in a relationship with someone who's supportive, kind, and loving, you'll believe you're worthy of love and affection.

    - On the other hand, if one or more of your major relationships causes you to feel hurt, discouraged, disappointed, or angry, your self-esteem probably suffers because of it.

    - Are most of the people you're close to positive and encouraging toward you? Do you feel emotionally supported by them? ***When you fill your life with loving, caring people, it will make it easier for you to maintain healthy self-esteem.***

4. **Take action to change relationships that bring you down.** Tell the person how you feel when they speak negatively toward you, and then share what you want the person to do instead.

    - "It hurts my feelings when you call me, 'Chubby.' I'd like you to call me by my name instead." You could also say something like, "When you yell at me, I get scared. Can you please lower your voice or wait until you're not angry before you talk to me?"

- There may be times when you must make a decision to end the relationship for your own best interests. If you feel unhappy more than you feel happy about being with a person, it's wise to consider moving on to a more emotionally uncluttered existence.

- Nothing will bring down your self-esteem quicker than a relationship filled with negativity and angst.

Having a cluttered home or emotional state can hamper your efforts to build self-esteem. Take action to bring order into your life. Evaluate close personal relationships and work to resolve any that are messy or chaotic. **Clean up your act in every way and you'll feel better about you.**

Plus, when you find yourself without chaos, you can better focus on the life you've always wanted.

> "Remember always that you not only have the right to be an individual, you have an obligation to be one."
>
> **- Eleanor Roosevelt**

Immerse Yourself in Hobbies and Activities You Love

Part of stoking your self-esteem is allowing yourself the time, space, and supplies to just be you - to enjoy taking part in the activities that you choose.

If you've found yourself feeling angry, resentful, or just empty lately, maybe it's time to get back into doing what you love to do.

1. **Recognize that doing something you love ignites your passion for life.** You tend to be good at things you like to do. People will praise your efforts. You'll feel great about doing what you love. In essence, your self-esteem can be found by doing your special pastime.

2. **Focus your efforts.** Rather than trying three new activities or hobbies you want to explore, *pick one that you get excited about.* Then, channel your efforts into that hobby. You'll see yourself getting better and better, and it will feel marvelous!

3. **Schedule "fun time" into your appointment book.** When you do what you love on a regular basis (at least once weekly), your interest and excitement in the activity is piqued. You have something to look forward to. You want to learn more and do more. It's exhilarating. There's no easier way to get excited about life than to get into something you really want to do.

How can you not feel better about yourself when you're taking part in activities you adore? When you do those things, you develop more passion in your life. Immerse yourself into your beloved hobbies and you will truly enhance your self-esteem.

"The privilege of a lifetime is being who you are."

- Joseph Campbell

Concentrate on Being a Great Partner or Parent

When you demonstrate who the most important people in your life are, something wonderful happens. The relationships bloom, and so does your self-esteem.

Review the strategies below to increase your efforts to be a fabulous partner or parent and in turn, cultivate your self-esteem and happiness:

1. **Notice what you're good at in your role as a partner or parent.** Pat yourself on the back. Recognizing your strengths in your relationship will help you realize what a giving, caring person you are.

2. **Decide what you can do to improve as a partner, mother, or father.** And then do it. Perhaps you could deepen your relationships with your kids by spending one-on-one time with each of them every week. In your partner relationship, bring some romance to the time you spend together to reignite sparks and keep the fires of romantic passion burning.

3. **Find the joy in your role.** What is it about being a mom, dad, wife, husband, or partner that makes you happy? Recognize there was a time in your life when you likely yearned to be in the very role you now have. Take some time to find the real satisfaction and joy in your important life role(s).

   - Immerse yourself in the joy of the stage of life you find yourself in right now. Notice the attraction you feel toward your partner. Smile at your child's sweet ways. Recognize all that is good, fresh, and true around you.

4. **Identify with your gratitude for your partner or children.** It's easy to get caught up in the whirlwind of working and

paying the bills. Take some moments to give thanks for those special people in your life. When you recognize the fascinating, loving people you have close to you, you'll realize you must be a pretty worthy person, too.

5. **Refuse to take your relationship for granted.** Stay in tune emotionally with the people closest to you. Notice their wants and needs. Be there for that special someone as much as you can.

- When you connect with the fact that neither of you really have to be where you are, you can see that you each chose the other. And that's pretty awesome, don't you think?

Focusing your efforts to be the best partner or parent you can be will bring incredible feelings of passion, joy, and self-satisfaction to your life. Figure out what you're good at and determine the areas you need to work on. See the fun and joy in your role.

Let yourself feel thankful and vow to never take your relationship for granted. Your self-esteem will bloom.

> *"Tell me how a person judges his or her self-esteem and I will tell you how that person operates at work, in love, in sex, in parenting, in every important aspect of existence - and how high he or she is likely to rise. The reputation you have with yourself - your self-esteem - is the single most important factor for a fulfilling life."*
>
> *- Nathaniel Branden*

Recognize Physical Well-Being is Intimately Connected with Your Self-Esteem

The state of your physical self is an integral aspect to how you feel about yourself. *Think about the time, effort, and money you put into your physical appearance.* Regular haircuts, professional shaves, facials, manicures, pedicures, and nice clothes are investments, not only in your appearance, but in your self-esteem as well.

Try these tips for keeping up your physical appearance to build your self-esteem:

1. **Take part in regular physical activity at least four times a week.** Exercising five or six times weekly is even better.
   - When you exercise consistently you look better. Your skin is clearer. Your eyes are brighter. You appear more toned. And you walk with a certain renewed sense of confidence.

2. **Become good at one sport.** Read about it. Study it. Practice it. Make it your "thing." When you do, you'll feel physically stronger. *And when you feel physically stronger, your confidence thrives.*
   - People will come to you and ask for your advice on the sport. You'll feel proud about what you know and how you excel.

3. **Discover a hairstyle or haircut that's exactly right for you.** A good barber or hairdresser can help. Rather than continually try to change your hair to go with the trends, instead, find the right cut for you that consistently looks great.

4. **Take care of your skin.** Whether you're male or female, take care of your skin, especially your face.

- Check out the cosmetics counter at a local department store and inquire about an effective skin care regimen. Don't forget some body lotion for your arms and legs, too.

5. **Wear well-fitting, classic clothing.** Your clothes don't have to be expensive, but they should fit and flatter your body. If you struggle to select the styles that look best on you, ask for help when you're shopping. Or seek assistance from a friend who always looks fantastic.

- Even a small wardrobe of 8-10 high quality, nice-fitting pieces that mix and match can make you feel really great about yourself.

You've probably suspected that how you care for yourself physically is connected with how you feel overall about yourself. Take pride in how you appear physically and your self-esteem will grow.

"Regardless of how you feel inside, always try to look like a winner. Even if you are behind, a sustained look of control and confidence can give you a mental edge that results in victory."

- Arthur Ashe

Rejoice in Your Uniqueness

When you recognize your special sense of uniqueness and fully accept every part of yourself, you have successfully embraced the essence of you. And when you do, you'll have achieved great comfort and satisfaction with yourself.

Reflect on these strategies to move ahead in your quest for self-esteem:

1. **Identify that there is only one you.** That's right: no one else on this Earth is quite like you. Your one-of-a-kind blend of character traits isn't repeated by anyone else.

2. **Take note of your unique mix of talents and skills.** Maybe you're a highly talented artist or musician and can wash a car or mow the lawn quicker than anybody else on your block.

    - You love to tell stories and your friends always call you to seek advice on how to deal with challenges with their friends.

    - *Write down every talent and skill you believe you have.* Then enjoy the glory of all the great things you can do. Let yourself feel marvelous about what's on your list.

3. **Acknowledge the compliments you receive from others.** Learn to be open and accepting of what others tell you that you do really well. If you pay attention, your friends and loved ones will mention what you're fantastic at through the compliments they give you.

    - Maybe you're the safest driver, funniest person to be around, or the best cook in your group of friends. When your friends remind you of these things, tell them you appreciate their comments. ***Let yourself feel the love.***

4. **Realize you've survived troubles before.** You've no doubt survived your own set of struggles to make it to where you are right now. So, thank your lucky stars for providing you with the skills and talents that can help you survive and thrive.

There's no one else quite like you, and that's something to feel good about. Notice your own mix of personality characteristics, talents, and skills. Bask in the compliments you receive from others. And rejoice about whatever you have that's good in your life.

> "The greatest difficulty is that men do not think enough of themselves, do not consider what it is that they are sacrificing when they follow in a herd, or when they cater for their establishment."
>
> *- Ralph Waldo Emerson*

Mindshift Conclusion

You enhance your passion for life whenever you increase your self-esteem. Some activities to take part in include applying yourself at work, using your thoughts to help yourself feel better, and doing some housecleaning, physically and emotionally. Also, take time to practice the hobbies and activities you love, and work to be the best partner or parent you can be.

Focus on sprucing up your physical self and allow yourself to feel joy about your special set of talents and skills—there is only one you.

As you begin working on these areas of your life, you'll notice something slowly flowering: your self-esteem! And when you have self-esteem, you're ready to build the life you crave and so richly deserve.

> "Think like a queen. A queen is not afraid to fail. Failure is another steppingstone to greatness."
>
> *- Oprah Winfrey*

Mindshift Six
Tap Into Your Intuition

☙

"Intuition enlightens and so links up with pure thought. They together become an intelligence which is not simply of the brain, which does not calculate, but feels and thinks."

- Piet Mondrian

As society becomes more evolved, there is a greater emphasis placed on processes, habits, logic, and mental toughness. Modern society can also feel a little empty and meaningless, too. We've been ignoring our intuition in order to fit in. We choose comfort over pursuing our purpose. **We choose a life that we think will impress others rather than living a life we find fulfilling.** Our intuition is a form of wisdom that is specific to us. Your intuition is different from your neighbor's. Your intuition can guide you to where you should be. You can call it a gut feeling, a connection to GOD, or a wisdom that you've developed throughout your lifetime. Regardless of how you want to describe it, everyone knows what intuition feels like. You have intuition, but have you been using it? Have you been training it?

In this Mindshift, you'll discover more about intuition, how to develop it further, and how to use it effectively.

What is Intuition?

There are many ways to view intuition depending on whom you ask. It also depends on the part of the world and the era. Intuition means different things to different people. Wikipedia defines intuition as, "the ability to acquire knowledge without recourse to conscious reasoning." Plato considered intuition to be derived from pre-existing knowledge that all people potentially have access to. This is along the idea of a shared consciousness. What one person knows is available to everyone, even across time. Freud had little to say about intuition, but made it clear he did not believe it was a viable means of acquiring knowledge or information. In modern times, there are also many differing opinions on intuition that range from the supernatural to the idea that intuition doesn't really exist. Others insist that intuition is the brain rapidly evaluating your current situation, your knowledge, values, goals, and past experiences to provide a recommendation. This recommendation is provided in the form of a physical sensation that varies from person to person.

How you choose to view your intuition is entirely up to you. But there's no doubt that most people do experience gut feelings, hunches, an instinct, a sixth sense, or an inkling. The real questions are: should you follow or reject your intuition, and how do you develop and use your intuition if you decide that it is valuable?

> *"We have no reason to expect the quality of intuition to improve with the importance of the problem. Perhaps the contrary: high-stake problems are likely to involve powerful emotions and strong impulses to action."*
>
> *- Daniel Kahneman*

Consider these topics as a way to learn more about intuition and how it can benefit your life

1. **What is Intuition?** There are many definitions of intuition. What is your definition? We'll present the most common ideas and let you choose for yourself.

2. **The Value of Intuition.** What can intuition do for you? Does it have any real value, or is it just another distraction to avoid?

3. **Obstacles to Intuition.** There are a multitude of things that can make accessing your intuition more challenging. This bullet point will provide the most common obstacles and effective solutions.

4. **Intuition-Boosting Exercises.** These exercises are sure to help you develop your intuition. You'll be challenged and amused as you implement these exercises. Train your intuition and see what happens.

5. **Using Your Intuition to Make Effective Decisions.** When the quality of your decisions improves, the quality of your life improves, too. Learn how to use your intuition to make beneficial choices.

6. **Using Your Intuition to Find Your Purpose in Life.** You've been misled by society and your urge to follow the norms. If you don't enjoy your life, this tip is for you. You can finally find your purpose in life.

7. **Tips to Use Daily to Enhance Your Intuition.** This final bullet point will provide some ways to bring using your intuition into your daily routines.

"As hackneyed and cliché as it sounds, follow your heart. We are all given intuition and instincts, and sometimes it is hard to follow those instincts with the fears and pressures that surround us - but you have to do it."

- Michael Feinstein

The Value of Intuition

Intuition has great value when used properly and regularly. **Your intuition is always available to you and can greatly enhance the quality of your life.** Once you understand the power of your intuition, you'll be sure to use it in your daily life to make positive changes in all aspects of your life.

See how your intuition can be of great benefit to you:

1. **Intuition can enable you to make wiser decisions.** There have been several studies demonstrating that people who include their intuition in the decision-making process make faster and higher quality decisions compared to those people who rely on logic alone. Imagine making better decisions in less time! The quality of your life is largely the result of the quality of your decisions. The world is very cause-effect in nature. *Your decisions are the cause, and your life is the effect.*

2. **Your intuition can help you to open up to new ideas.** When we rely on logic alone, we reject many ideas that should be given consideration. After a certain age, we tend to rely too much on what we know and reject that which is unfamiliar.

   - Intuition allows the unknown to become a possibility.

3. **Your intuitive voice can help you avoid disaster.** Think about all the times that your intuition saved you from doing some-

thing stupid. Then consider all the times you ignored your intuition and misery was the result.

- Our brains are very protective. Your subconscious will do all it can to help you avoid making a foolish choice.

4. **Your creativity will increase when you learn to use your intuition.** Creativity and intuition are closely related. Think about the most creative people you know. They are much more likely to follow their gut than to rely on logic and rationale.

5. **Your inttuition will help you to find your purpose.** Your intuition is trying to tell you what you should do with your life. It knows what you like and don't like. It understands the great potential you possess.

- Your true purpose in life isn't a secret to your intuition. Get in touch with your intuition, and you'll find your purpose.

6. **Your relationships are enhanced when you grow your intuition.** Your intuition doesn't just put you in touch with yourself; it also enhances your ability to read and respond to others in your life.

- You become much better at understanding others and noticing their emotional states.

- Your intuition will also help you to make more effective choices of how to react and relate to the people in your life.

7. **Relying on your intuition can boost your happiness.** Better choices lead to a better life. Your intuition allows you to avoid many of the avoidable challenges in life. Plus, finding and living your purpose can certainly add a lot to your happiness.

Your intuition is free and always available to you. **It has tremendous power when used appropriately.** Better decisions, greater levels of happiness, and increased creativity are just a few of the benefits you can expect to receive if you listen to your intuition on a regular basis.

"There is a universal, intelligent, life force that exists within everyone and everything. It resides within each one of us as a deep wisdom, an inner knowing. We can access this wonderful source of knowledge and wisdom through our intuition, an inner sense that tells us what feels right and true for us at any given moment."

- Shakti Gawain

Obstacles to Intuition

Your intuition is often quiet and subtle. **Distractions and stress are just two of the obstacles you'll face when learning how to tap into your intuition more fully.** Eliminating obstacles is an important part of becoming maximally effective at anything.

Remove these obstacles if you want to get the most from your intuition:

1. **Diet.** Your mind and body need to be operating well if you want to be able to sense your intuition clearly. Anything that negatively alters how you feel can throw off your intuition. A healthy diet is always the best policy. Think about the foods that don't work well for you. A few possibilities include:

    → Gluten

    → Sugar

    → Caffeine

- → Alcohol
- → Processed foods
- → Nuts
- → Shellfish

Notice how you feel after eating a food and make note of it for future reference. Avoid those foods that don't allow you to feel your best.

2. **Insufficient sleep.** Intuition is referred to as a gut feeling for a reason. It's a subtle feeling. It's subtle enough that you might not notice it if you're exhausted.

   - Get enough sleep if you want to tap into your intuition fully.

3. **Stress.** Stress can be another powerful blocker to intuition. Your mind is all over the place, and your body is stressed. The message that your intuition is trying to deliver might not be noticed in all the noise.

   - Learn how to relax. Experiment and see what works best for you.

4. **Doubt.** Intuition requires trust. If you keep ignoring your intuition, it might decide to stop trying to help you. Follow up on your intuition in a responsible manner.

   - Be brave and give your intuition a chance. Start small and grow from there.

5. **A lack of practice.** Practice reaching out to your intuition and noticing the messages it provides. You have to practice something to become good at it. Your intuition is not an exception.

- Use your intuition throughout the day. There are several suggestions later in this Mindshift.

6. **A need for certainty.** Certainty and intuition rarely go together. There's often a vagueness to intuition. If you need certainty, you'll rarely benefit from your intuition. Be prepared to act on less-than-complete information.

    - Give your intuition the benefit of the doubt. It's not necessary to understand everything in order to take the next step.

7. **Your preferences.** Our wishes can taint our intuition. For example, if you have the opportunity to date two people, but one is much more attractive than the other, your intuition might not be able to overpower your preference.

    - Our desire to have things be a certain way is always an obstacle to making a smart decision. Be open to new possibilities.

8. **A scattered mind.** If your mind is unsettled, tapping into your intuition may prove to be very challenging. A calm, centered, and relaxed mind is optimal.

    - Remove as many distractions and sources of stress from your life as you can. Only look to your intuition when you are relaxed and focused.

9. **Fear.** Fear is a major obstacle to intuition. For example, your intuition might be telling you to approach a particular person and strike up a conversation. However, your fear of rejection might be a more powerful force in your decision-making process than your intuition.

    - The only way to become bold is to move forward in spite of your fear.

You'll notice that many of these obstacles are common in life. **It's challenging to hear your intuition if you're suffering from financial stress, or if you have too many distractions in your life.** Review the obstacles in this bullet point and do your best to remove as many of them as possible from your life.

> *"Intuition is the key to everything, in painting, filmmaking, business - everything. I think you could have an intellectual ability, but if you can sharpen your intuition, which they say is emotion and intellect joining together, then a knowingness occurs."*
>
> ***- David Lynch***

Intuition-Boosting Exercises

If you want bigger muscles, you must train them. If you want to have a great memory, you have to train it. **Building your intuition requires training, too.** These exercises will begin the process of building your intuition, but you must use them to reap any benefits.

Boost your intuition with these fun and interesting exercises:

1. **People watch.** Go someplace with a lot of people that will also allow you to sit and watch. This could be a park, the mall, a bookstore, the beach, or any other place with many people and the ability to loiter for at least 30 minutes. Randomly pick someone and evaluate them using your intuition.

    - Are they wealthy, poor, or of average financial means?
    - Are they married, single, or in a relationship?
    - Do they have kids?
    - Do they look nice? Do they look unkind? What gives you that impression?

- What type of career do you think they most likely have?
- How old are they?
- What does their diet look like?
- What are their values?
- If the person is an appropriate age or gender, would you date them? Why or why not?
- Describe their personality.
- What is the basic vibe you get from this person?

2. **Analyze your dreams.** Your dreams are a peek into your subconscious. Keep a pad of paper and pen by your bed. Immediately upon waking up, do your best to recall your dreams. It takes very little time or activity before your ability to recall your dreams fades. So, remember as much as you can before you move.

    - Grab your pen and paper and write down your observations about your dreams. Include the details of the dream itself.
    - What happened and how did it make you feel?
    - What are your dreams trying to tell you?
    - How do your dreams relate to the current challenges in your life?
    - How do your dreams relate to the decisions you're facing?
    - What are the elements of your dreams that keep recurring over time?

3. **Notice your dream signs.** Dream signs are those aspects of your dreams that should tip you off that you're dreaming. The strangest things happen in dreams, but we rarely question

them. Learning your dream signs is a great way to develop your intuition. Record your dream signs. Here are a few common ones:

- The presence of someone that has died. If your deceased friend or relative is in a dream, that's a sure sign that you're dreaming.
- Unusual abilities. Can you suddenly do the splits, jump really high, fly, see through walls, or breathe underwater?
- Spontaneous changes in the environment. Dreams are far less static than you probably realize. If you look at a clock twice in a dream, it won't show the same time. People's clothing changes. The landscape changes. One minute it's daytime, the next it's dark.
- Impossible things. Monsters, 500-pound dogs, a car that converts into a jet, a flying house, or an elephant the size of a mouse.
- Unusual actions or circumstances. Are you being chased by a group of people? Are you shooting a gun at bad guys? Are you racing a car? Are you visiting the pyramids of Egypt? Are you late for your high school math class, but you haven't attended high school for 30 years?
- Changes to your regular life. Are you driving a different car than normal? Is your house different? Is your hair longer? Are you heavier or lighter? Is your workplace different?
- You'll notice recurring signs that should allow you to notice that you're dreaming. Record all of your dream signs and look for patterns.

- Controlling your dreams can greatly increase your insight and intuition.

4. **Three cards.** Take three index cards and write "Yes" on the first, "No" on the second, and "Maybe" on the last card. Spread the cards out in front of you with the writing facing up.

    - Ask yourself a question that you know to be true. For example, "Do I drive a blue car?"

    - Hold one hand over the "Yes" card and notice how that feels. Describe the feeling. Do you feel warm, cold, pressure, openness, or constriction? Do you feel it in your head, chest, gut, or some combination? Do your hands tingle? Notice all of the physical sensations you experience.

    - Repeat the process by holding your hand over the "No" and then the "Maybe" cards. Notice how each one feels to you.

    - Repeat the experiment by asking yourself a question that is a certain "No," and then again with a "Maybe" question.

    - Begin using the process as part of your decision-making process. Follow your intuition as much as possible and see what happens.

5. **Traffic light.** This is similar to the three-card process but doesn't require the use of any physical props. Everything occurs in your mind.

    - Ask yourself a "Yes," "No," or "Maybe" question just like before.

    - Immediately after asking the question, visualize a traffic light and notice the color of the light shining.

    - Green=Yes. Yellow=Maybe. Red=No.

- Do this with questions that have obvious answers so you can verify that the process is working for you.
- Use the process in your daily life and make note of the results.

6. **Take a walk.** This is a great way to enhance all of your senses. Go for a walk. Anywhere will do.
   - Begin by focusing entirely on your sense of sight. Notice everything you can see. Notice every squirrel, car, cloud, and blade of grass. However, avoid making commentary on what you see.
   - Avoid saying to yourself, "Awww, what a cute dog. He reminds me of my childhood dog, Buddy."
   - Use your peripheral vision and take in as much as you can.
   - Next, use your hearing. Obviously, you need to pay enough attention to what you're seeing to avoid stepping in front of a car or tripping. However, the focus is now on your hearing. Hear every distant and close sound your ears can pick up.
   - Feeling. What do you physically feel during your walk? Heat? Cold? Wind blowing across your skin or through your hair? Pressure on the bottoms of your feet? Tightness in your back? Pain? The discomfort of the sun in your eyes?
   - Smell. Repeat the process with your sense of smell. Turn your head and catch every scent you can. What do you smell?
   - Taste. This last sense is more limited within the context of a walk but give it a try. When you get home, eat something with a mixture of flavors, such as a salad or a complex soup. Notice the individual flavors.

7. **Take an intuitive drive.** Hop in the car and ask your intuition which way to turn. Every time you come to a possible turning point, ask yourself, "Which way should I go? Should I turn here or keep going straight?" See where you end up. Be open to your intuition's direction.

8. **Spend more time in nature.** We spend a lot of time in an artificial world. Buildings, cars, electronic devices, roads, noise, and pollution. It's easy for your intuition to become overwhelmed by it all.

    - Spend some time just sitting in the woods enjoying the trees, plants, and animals.
    - It's also easier to notice the signals your intuition is trying to send you in a natural and peaceful environment.

9. **Skip the daily routine.** Routines can be very useful. They require minimal brain power and allow us to accomplish a lot in a short period of time. However, routines can override any signal your intuition could be trying to send you.

    - Give yourself a day as free from routines as possible. Decide what to do next by using your intuition.

10. **Read.** Intuition is a popular and interesting topic. Read all that you can on the subject. Teach yourself all that you can and practice what you learn.

11. **Review your past.** Your past is full of great examples of following and ignoring your intuition.

    - Start with your greatest victories and failures. Do your best to remember when you made the decisions that led to those successes and failures. Did you follow or ignore your intuition? In general, has your intuition been right or wrong?

- Did you date the right people for you?
- Did you choose a college and major that worked well for you?
- Did you choose a career you enjoy?
- Have you chosen friends that provide a positive, beneficial relationship?
- Have you made effective financial decisions?

You have to train to become great at something, whether it's playing the piano, mastering chess, or becoming a great public speaker. Your intuition requires training, too. **Or more correctly, you require training to access your intuition effectively.** Your intuition is actually just fine as it is.

> *"Some people say there's nothing new under the Sun. I still think that there's room to create, you know. And intuition doesn't necessarily come from under this Sun. It comes from within."*
>
> **- Pharrell Williams**

Using Your Intuition to Make Effective Decisions

It's all about making smart decisions, isn't it? Choosing the wrong spouse, the wrong foods to eat, or the wrong career has a huge impact on your life. But it's not just the big decisions that cause us grief. It's all the little decisions each day that move our lives toward a better, or worse, place. If your life doesn't please you, the most effective thing you can do is to stop making poor decisions. **A few effective decisions and time are all that you need to enhance your life significantly.**

See how to use your intuition to make great decisions:

1. **Get clear.** Relieve yourself of all the opinions, beliefs, values, and ideas of others. These have nothing to do with you. Your decisions have to be right for you. Leave others to worry about their own decisions.

    - If your decision is based even 1% on what others will think, you're playing a losing game.

2. **Get clear, Part Two.** Let go of your own opinions. Release your fears. Ignore your need for comfort. Ignore the beliefs you have about yourself. Reject everything that is not important to you.

3. **Clearly define the decision that needs to be made and your options.** Perhaps you are trying to decide if you should rent an apartment, versus buying a house, versus buying a condo.

4. **Find a quiet spot and close your eyes.** Imagine making each of those choices and notice how it feels.

    - Imagine deciding that you're going to rent an apartment. How does that feel? What are the physical sensations you're experiencing? What thoughts are you thinking? What emotions are you feeling?
    - Take a few deep breaths and complete the process with the other options.

5. **Your decision should be very clear to you.** The right decision will feel peaceful. You might feel excited. A clear "no" feels the same as thinking about eating a food you dislike. It's a clenched, restricted feeling.

If you fail to find a solution that feels right, find additional options or work further on releasing yourself from the influence of others. It's also possible that you have a limiting view of yourself or life in general. The first two steps of this process are challenging, but crucial. Imagine that all choices are just as right as any of the others. Allow your intuition to guide your decisions.

> *"The comfort zone is the great enemy to creativity; moving beyond it necessitates intuition, which in turn configures new perspectives and conquers fears."*
>
> *- Dan Stevens*

Using Your Intuition to Find Your Purpose in Life

There is a part of you that understands who you are and what you're supposed to be doing. Your intuition can be the mechanism by which you become aware of this information. You've probably tried to find your purpose using more rational means. You have thought, pondered, and evaluated. Perhaps you've come up with a choice that doesn't feel right for you or never reached a conclusion at all.

Use these strategies to let your intuition help you find your purpose in life:

1. **How do you feel about your current situation?** Be clear on what you like and don't like about your current situation. Include the following in your assessment:
   - Finances
   - Relationships
   - Career
   - Hobbies
   - Health
2. **Ask yourself, "What do I need to feel happy and fulfilled?"** Find a quiet place when you're feeling relaxed and open. Ask yourself the above question and listen to the answer.

- Be focused on what you need, rather than what you want. Wants are often ego-driven and get in the way of what you need. You might want a jet or a yacht, but those things are not needs, and they get in the way of living your purpose more than they help.

- You might, for example, decide that you need $50,000 per year, three good friends, a dog, a piano, and a career that focuses on helping the environment.

3. **Examine how fear is limiting your life.** Fear has controlled your life more than you think. It has limited your education, career, relationships, hobbies, travel, and all of the other aspects of your life.

    - Imagine what your life would look like today if you had not allowed fear to impact your choices over the years.

    - If you were fearless in growing your career, you might be in a different place professionally and financially.

    - Projecting what your life could have been without fear demonstrates how far your intuition could have taken you, if you had permitted your intuition to direct your life instead of your fear.

4. **What do you love to do?** Find a quiet place again and ask yourself what you love to do. Ask yourself when you have felt most fulfilled. Be quiet and really focus on the answers you receive.

5. **Ask your intuition to reveal your purpose to you.** The previous steps were just a warmup. This is where things become relevant.

- Do more than just find a quiet place in your home. Get out of the house and find some solitude. It can be a spot in the woods. It could be a hotel room. It can be anywhere you are alone and feel comfortable, but it needs to be someplace outside of your familiar territory.

- Close your eyes, take a deep breath, and tell your intuition to reveal your purpose to you. Listen to what it says.

6. **How did the response you received feel to you?** It should feel "right," even if it feels illogical or challenging. Your purpose does not have to be something that's easy for you. In fact, it might be the most challenging thing you've ever done.

   - However, **it should be exciting, interesting, and important to you.** It might not be something that impresses other people. This is your purpose, not someone else's.

7. **Start making a plan.** We've all had great ideas that we failed to pursue. Your purpose is too important to leave to chance. Start making a plan that will allow you to immediately begin pursuing your purpose.

A life without purpose can feel like a slow, painful death. You were not created to go to a job you don't like. **You aren't designed to spend your time in the same way as everyone else.** Find your purpose and make your life interesting again.

> *"I write as if I were drunk. It is a process of intuition rather than placing myself above my story like a puppeteer pulling strings. For me, it's a scary, chaotic process over which I have little control. Words demand other words, characters resist me."*
>
> *- Elif Safak*

Tips to Use Daily to Enhance Your Intuition

There are little things you can do each day to boost your intuition. **Enhancing your intuition doesn't have to take a lot of time if you work on it each day.** A little work can go a long way when applied consistently with a strong intention. Include your intuition in your daily routines if you want to get the most from it.

Use these tips to practice using your intuition each and every day:

1. **Make use of repetitive tasks.** There are certain tasks that allow our minds to wander. A few of these include mowing grass, taking a shower, washing dishes, and vacuuming the carpet.

    - These types of activities keep your conscious mind occupied at a low level. This allows your subconscious a better opportunity to make itself heard.

2. **Use solitude and quiet when they are available.** View these times as opportunities to use your intuition. Avoid allowing these opportunities to slip through your fingers.

3. **Find the best time of day to reach out to your intuition.** You might find that just before falling asleep and immediately after waking up are ideal times for you. You might also find these to be the worst times! Experiment and see if one time of day is more effective.

4. **Differentiate between your intuition and your preferences.** This is very challenging. For example, your natural inclination might be to choose a candy bar over a salad. However, it's clear that the salad is the better choice. You might think that your intuition is screaming for you to have the candy bar, but it is not!

    - During those times that the right choice is abundantly clear, you might have to rely on the logical choice. You don't need your intuition to tell you not to use drugs, to eat healthily, or to exercise instead of sitting on the couch.

5. **Use your intuition regularly.** Use your intuition as much as you can. It can be choosing what variety of toothpaste to purchase or deciding how to spend your weekend. Use your intuition and watch it grow before your eyes.

6. **Be aware of your intuition at all times.** Your intuition speaks to you even when you don't actively engage with it. It is sending you messages even when you don't ask it a question. You have to pay attention, or you might miss out on something important.

7. **Have a creative hobby.** This is a great time for your intuition to speak up. You could choose to write, paint, play an instrument, arrange flowers, or even scrapbook.

8. **Test your intuition.** Ask your intuition where your lost car keys are located. See if your intuition knows who's going to win the football game. Maybe your intuition can figure out whether your friend is going to have a baby boy or girl.

9. **Take care of your basic needs.** Eat well, get enough sleep, and see your doctor regularly. How well will your intuition work after getting only three hours of sleep, eating a burrito from the gas station, and suffering from multiple health ailments? Intuition works best from a neutral position: well-rested, relaxed, and healthy.

"Intuition is the very force or activity of the soul in its experience through whatever has been the experience of the soul itself."

- Henry Reed

Mindshift Conclusion

Your intuition is the result of your past experiences and all of your knowledge. If you believe Plato, your intuition is a link to all the knowledge of a collective consciousness.

Regardless of how you choose to view intuition, your intuition is a powerful tool that is available to you when making decisions. Intuition can be vague, quiet, and gentle. This is why intention and practice are required to get the most from this important part of you. Rather than choosing to follow the choices that the rest of society is making, it is time to do what is right for you, no matter how unique it might be. Use your intuition when making decisions in your life. The best answer for someone else is not always the best answer for you.

Mindshift Seven
Master Your Day

☙

What if you could finally master your time? You would see yourself make more, have more time with your family, and achieve more. By managing time effectively, you will experience less stress and a better sense of stability in your daily life. Thinking through the details of your day, from the places you work to the routines you implement, will provide a secure structure. *This enables you to let go of thinking about unnecessary details in order to focus on what is truly important to you.* These strategies will help you make the most use of your time and be the most productive.

Consider this overview of tools to better manage your time and be more productive:

- **Optimizing Productivity with Time and Space.** Visualize your ideal workspace and consider ways to make it a reality. In order to make the most use of time, think about when the most productivity takes place in your day.

- **Focused Task Management.** There are surprising disadvantages to multitasking, context switching, and task switching. Though it may seem impressive to do many tasks at once, you'll actually be more productive if you focus on just one thing at a time.

- **Prioritizing Daily Tasks.** How do you decide on the most important tasks? Discover how to get the most out of work time by focusing on the highest-priority tasks.

- **Pay Attention to Your Time.** What does it mean to be mindful? If you can focus on the present moment, you will be fully invested in the task at hand.

- **Setting Up Your Daily System.** Look at the big picture and then focus on the day-to-day reality of making goals come to fruition.

- **Set a Schedule, Stick to it.** Consider how you want each hour of your day to flow and create a realistic structure to follow.

Optimizing Productivity with Time and Space

Using effective time management techniques provides stability and consistency to daily life. As a result, you'll spend less time worrying about the future and more time focusing on the task at hand.

The first thing to consider in mapping out your day is your peak productivity time. Next, think about *where* you're most productive. As you visualize your whole day, you are more able to focus on the small pieces.

Schedule Your Time to Shine

In order to effectively manage your hour-by-hour and day-by-day routine, you must first ask yourself, *"What is the time of day that I most thrive?"* Think for a moment about how your most ideal productive day would go. Do you take the morning slow? Do you get right into work? Are you most productive at night?

Once you can pinpoint your most productive hours, you're better able to work out the rest of your day, so you can make the most out of your valuable time.

Perhaps you've found that it is difficult to get productive at all during the day. This frustrating dilemma is one that you can overcome. Though it may be a struggle to get going, once you're in the flow of your work, all will come easily.

Times of Optimal Productivity:

- A 2017 California-based research study found that **the most productive time of day is around 11:00 am.**

- **People are most mentally alert between 9:00 am and 11:00 am.** You can use this information while scheduling meetings, as this is the time where people will be the most attentive.

- Information has even been found about the months where people are most productive. **The most productive month of the year is typically October.**

As you walk through the typical layout of your day, picture the parts you might want to change. Perhaps there are daily time management habits that you'd like to get rid of. Maybe you have multiple times throughout the day where you find yourself in a productive state.

If you can picture your productivity in 90-minute increments, it might make it easier to place those throughout your day or all in one block.

What if I only have a limited amount of time?

Because life is life, there will always be distractions or needs that are unplanned. If you planned to have four hours to work, but you wind up only having one hour, that does not mean the day or the time to be productive has to be completely lost. It can be easy to have an all-or-nothing mindset when it comes to following a schedule, but flexibility is key.

If you cannot do all of it, do some of it.

Once the schedule has been thrown off, it can seem like the rest of the day will be negatively affected as well. This doesn't need to be the case. In order to make the most of your time all the time, take the hour you have and do everything you can with it. You do not need to rush.

Choose your highest-priority task first. Assign yourself an hour of working on what will move the needle the most, whatever will move you ahead the furthest.

Try these tips to make the most out of a limited amount of time:

- **Take it one minute at a time.** An hour may not seem like a long time. However, a lot can happen in 10 minutes.
- It can be easy to let an entire hour fly by without having done anything. Minimize distractions. Turn your phone on silent. Focus on exactly what is in front of you.
- **Focus on tasks that will move you the most toward your goal in the time you have.**
- Prioritize the tasks that need the most immediate attention.

The Places That Inspire You

When considering the time of day that you're most productive, you must also consider where you are when you're most productive.

Now, **envision the setting of your ideal, most productive workplace.** Look around. Are there others around you? What does it sound like? Is it a casual or a formal setting?

Perhaps you have a favorite coffee shop where you go to work. Make a regular habit of going to that place at your most productive time of day. If you're not able to get to your ideal setting, create an atmosphere with other qualities that reflect an ideal work setting.

Consider these ideas for places to work:

- **Go to a coffee shop.** Your favorite coffee shop can provide a comfortable and productive familiarity. A coffee shop is a great place to get out of isolation and be around people without being directly interrupted.

- **Join a coworking space.** Many cities have coworking spaces. A coworking space has all of the amenities of a typical workplace. You can enjoy some great motivation by surrounding yourself with others who are productive.

- **Your office.** If you already work in an office setting, look around the office to see if you can work in your favorite spot. Or, set up your desk to reflect your work needs. If you need minimal distractions, take all distracting items off your desk.

- **Outside.** Refresh yourself and your mind with nature. Find a table in the shade and **take in nature while diving into a productive state.**

- **At your house.** If you have a workspace where you live, you can add and remove setting elements according to your ideal environment. Be sure to keep your workspace away from where you sleep. Save your bedroom just for sleeping!

Whom will you work with?

Humans are social animals. Some are more social than others. If you find that other people give you energy, consider that fact in choosing where you work. Perhaps you're a social person, but not productive while being social.

Be honest with yourself and **make a decision based on how you use your time best.** If you have one person or a group of people that you work well around, invite them for a weekly work session and use that time to inspire yourself.

Establishing your best work time and setting will propel you to more effective time management. Asking the simple questions of *when* and *where* will enable you to create the structure that will handle the rest of your day.

Having this environment in place will anchor you to your schedule when obstacles and distractions arise.

Focused Task Management

While working on three things at time, it can feel like you're getting a lot done. Sometimes a mindset can occur that tells you, *"The more you are doing at once, the more you are getting done."* This thinking is false. In fact, the opposite is true.

When you focus on just one thing at a time, you'll achieve higher quality results. Having one thing that you're working on will free up more time. Moving from one thing to another or focusing on many things at once are two ineffective ways to manage time.

You may find yourself beginning a long to-do list, jumping from task to task. At the end of an hour, you may find that you have attempted many tasks but accomplished none.

There are three obstacles that may come up during your day. They all can adversely affect time management in different ways. These obstacles are multitasking, task switching, and context switching.

Multitasking

Multitasking involves doing many tasks at once that are all related to the same end result. Many people attempt multitasking in an effort to be efficient. In fact, it's often celebrated! However, multitasking is not as effective as some believe.

If you think you're an expert multitasker, think again.

For example, you may have experienced walking while trying to type and email on your phone. While these are both tasks that you know well, they become much more difficult when they're done at the same time. This is because your attention is split between two tasks instead of focused on one.

Task Switching

Task switching is similar to multitasking in that it involves doing many things at once. However, task switching is even less productive than multitasking. **Task switching occurs while focusing on many things at once that are *not related to one specific goal.***

For example, you may have a conversation on the phone about an upcoming event while writing an outline for a new project. These tasks have nothing to do with each other.

You are more likely to miss important details when you're trying to give your attention to two different things at once.

It can be difficult to focus. Task switching makes it even harder. The focused feeling of losing track of time and being in the zone is invigorating and productive. The habit of task switching inhibits the ability to get totally lost in your work. Switching from task to task simultaneously means that none of the work produced will be as high quality as the work done while focusing solely on one thing.

There are two types of task switching: interrupted task switching and rapid task switching.

Interrupted Task Switching

Interrupted task switching occurs most of the time when you have email, social media, and text message notifications.

If you have noise alerts or pop-ups on your computer, you'll likely be easily distracted and pulled out of the moment you are having with your work. If you're in a flow state, totally focused and even enjoying yourself, that can all be lost with a simple notification.

An example of this unfortunate interruption is illustrated by our biggest distraction: **social media**. Once you notice a new social media notification, the moment you click on it, you have officially task switched. You may be working on the project in one window while checking social media on the next.

These interruptions are a major obstacle in time management. **They inhibit you from entering the flow state required to get done what you need.**

Rapid Task Switching

Rapid task switching involves switching from task to task in rapid succession. Taking notes on your notebook with your computer open to another task is one surefire way to fall into rapid task switching. You may move from typing an email to writing an outline for a project you're working on in the same second.

Going from task to task in quick succession diminishes awareness not just of your work, but of the rest of the world around you as well. It limits your ability to think clearly and with care.

Context Switching

Context switching occurs when we go from one task to an entirely different task. This is different from multitasking and task switching in that it does not involve doing many tasks at once.

Context switching means moving from one project to another without completing either project. If you have eight hours in your work time, choose your most important project and work on that. In order to use your time most effectively, complete that first project before moving on to anything else. If you move from Project A before it is done, you'll likely end up with two unfinished projects by the end of the day, instead of one whole task done.

A huge disadvantage to context switching is that it wastes precious work time. **Once you've come out of focus, it takes about 25 minutes to get into another state of focus**. If you switch contexts three times in your day, you've lost over an hour of time that could have been expertly well spent.

Strategies

Have no fear. Though there are many things that come up, and there is so much to get done with so little time, it is possible to prevent these distracting habits.

Use these strategies to focus on just one thing at a time:
1. **Implement the when and where of your work environment.** When you're in your ideal work setting, you are more likely to become engulfed in your work.

2. **Make it a rule to complete a task before you begin the next one.** This will increase your work endurance and will help you get more done. You won't waste such precious time.

3. **Turn off all of your social media and email notifications.** Set all of your technology to the "*Do Not Disturb*" mode. You can even have an automated message that lets people know when you'll be back online.

4. **Stay away from distracting websites.** You may have a habit of typing in your favorite website when you really meant to check your email. You can avoid this by using applications and reminders that will protect you from distracting websites.

5. **Take advantage of sound.** Put on your favorite background noise or eliminate background noise altogether with noise-canceling headphones.

Prioritizing Daily Tasks

Mastering time management does not come easily; it takes practice and consistency. **The best way to ensure that you get everything done on your list is to prioritize the most important tasks and do them first.**

Prioritization skills come with practice. It may not always be clear what exactly is most important. Though some projects have steps, others are more general and can be accomplished in a variety of ways. Pick out the tasks that are most sure to move you forward.

Ask yourself, "If I complete this task, will I be satisfied with what I have done?" Consider the item that you would do, if you could only choose one thing to do. **Which task would move you closer to your goal in the allotted time?**

It can be difficult to know where to start when it comes to prioritizing a to-do list full of important tasks. You can begin the process by talking with others about how they prioritize their work. You can also look at your old habits.

Consider whether your current work habits are sustainable. Do you find yourself with many incomplete tasks during the week? Do you miss deadlines? These might be signs that you need to look at the big picture and reprioritize your items.

Follow this proven process to prioritize your tasks:

1. **Start by making a list of everything you need to do.** You can make a list that covers the entire week, and then break it down into day-by-day sections.

2. **Write any deadlines or time constraints while observing your list.** This will help you determine when you need to start working on what. Be sure to consider the size of each project and deadline.

3. **The night before each work day, look at your list and visualize your day.** What are the tasks that you can get done in your designated work time?

4. **Set aside tasks that are unnecessary or not pertinent to what you're currently trying to get done.** Look at how you want to spend the day and set aside tasks that do not relate to the objectives you have for your day.

5. **It's helpful to start on the most dreadful or difficult task first.** If you first accomplish something that you don't want to do, you'll feel less burdened and more motivated.

6. **You can use all of these things to set your priorities straight.** Take a step back and weigh the importance of each task according to the goals you have in mind.

Remain Flexible

There are bound to be distractions. New things pop up, surprises occur, and important phone calls come in. Even though you planned out your day the night before, there are days when nothing goes as planned, or things get pushed back.

When these unexpected turns occur, you can use your priorities to guide you toward the tasks to focus on when you do have time. If you have an impending deadline or particularly difficult task, begin with those. If you're asked to take on too much, practice boundaries and avoid promising more than you can deliver.

Use Your Time Wisely

Carefully consider your high-priority items as you look at each day. **Take advantage of your most productive hours by doing the items that need your utmost attention.** Use your time wisely by knowing how things are going to go and giving care to each minute.

Pay Attention to Your Time

There are 1,440 minutes in each day. Most people are awake for about 16 hours out of the day. **That means you have about 960 minutes to do what you need to do in order to have a successful day.** This may seem daunting, and it may seem inspiring. Regardless, it's important to be cognizant of the ways you spend your time.

On average, humans are able to focus for about 20 minutes at a time. However, it's possible to be focused for 20 minutes and then repeatedly refocus.

You can use this information to your advantage when you estimate how long each task will take. If something will take four hours, look at it in 20-minute sections. How much of this project can you get done in 20 minutes? How much can you get done in one hour?

Take Planned Breaks

Maintain your attention on each task, but be sure to take a break every 90 minutes. If 90 minutes seems too long, you can also take a break every 50 minutes. 15 to 20 minutes is a perfect length of time to give your brain a refreshing break.

You can practice being mindful of your time by being mindful during your timed breaks. Practicing a quick mindfulness activity is more effective than taking a break to get on social media or read the news.

Mindfulness enables you to calm your mind and come to the present moment. Social media stimulates the mind and distracts from the present moment.

Try these mindfulness activities during work breaks:

1. **Meditate.** You can meditate for just a few minutes. Sit up straight in your chair. Close your eyes or focus on one point ahead of you. Start to simply pay attention to your breath. Notice, "I am inhaling, I am exhaling."

2. **Go on a walk.** Embrace the feeling of fresh air and sunshine by taking a step away from your work and going on a walk. Leave your phone behind. Simply observe and notice the greenery, the sounds of cars, and the color of the sky.

3. **Take a coloring break.** Grab a coloring break and set a timer for 10 minutes. Use those minutes to relax and color. This exercise will help keep your mind engaged without thinking about other things.

4. **Notice your five senses.** Take a moment to notice all of your senses. What do you hear, see, smell, taste, and feel? Go through all of your muscle groups and relax them, starting with your toes and ending with your ears.

Set Reminders: Check Yourself

Set reminders for yourself to help notify you of an upcoming transition in your day. These small alerts can serve as a line of accountability when you're trying to practice new habits.

If you notice a "ding" five minutes before it's time to move on to your next task, you'll be able to find a stopping point and make a smooth transition to the next item of business.

You can also take advantage of the opportunity that an alert presents.

Use a small moment in your transition to acknowledge your day and check that your focus is on the task at hand. You don't always have to stop what you're doing in order to be mindful. You can take advantage of moments at work where you can bring your attention to exactly what you're doing.

If your next task calls for movement, bring your focus to your walking. Feel the ground beneath your shoes and focus on your breath, even if just for a moment.

It's easy to look to the future and concern ourselves with imagined scenarios that we truly cannot predict. **These small moments of mindfulness can provide a chance to let go of worry and focus on the task at hand without disrupting your day.**

How Does Mindfulness Affect Productivity?

An ability to focus on the present moment brings about a stronger connection to the task at hand rather than your entire to-do list. Those who practice mindfulness have been shown to be less affected by distractions.

Mindfulness increases productivity by creating a manageable stream of thoughts that do not overwhelm. By practicing mindfulness regularly, you're likely to increase your ability to regulate emotions. This stability provides focus solely on the thoughts that count.

Treat your time with care and attention. The best way to be mindful of your time is to be aware and conscious of what you do and when you do it. You can do this by creating a system, or a routine, for each day.

Setting Up Your Daily System

Time management isn't just about getting stuff done. **Time management is about structure and consistency.**

Structure provides a sense of security and relief to each day. It decreases the need for worry or time-wasting thoughts. If you already know how the first three hours of your day are going to go, you don't need to wake up and wonder how the next three hours will go. You'll already know, because you have a system.

Follow a Routine

Working within a structure, no matter how subtle, provides numerous benefits. **By having a routine, you're more likely to not just be more productive, but also to feel better all around.** You'll get more sound sleep, feel less stressed, and have a stronger ability to focus on each task at each designated time of day.

You can begin thinking about your routine by splitting your day into sections.

Begin with the first hour. What does the first hour of your day look like? **Try to spend the first hour of your day *off technology*.** Avoid checking your email or responding to text messages. Take the first hour of your day just for yourself, so you can transition into your day.

By preparing, thinking through, and strategizing for the day ahead, you'll feel a greater sense of stability.

Ask yourself these questions about your routine:

1. **Morning Routine**
   - What is the first thing you want to do each morning?
   - What is the second thing you want to do each morning?
   - What will make your morning feel like a success?
   - What is the most important daily task you'll do each morning?

2. **Nightly Routine**
   - How do you want to end your day?
   - How will you wind down from your day?
   - What is the most important task you want to do each night?
   - What task will help you feel a sense of completion about your day?

What are the most important things you want to get done in the morning? Accumulate small successes early on in your day. This will help you feel confident and ready for your day.

For example, you can start your day by making your bed. **Though this may seem insignificant, making your bed starts your day in a refreshingly successful way.** It lets you know that you're officially beginning your day, it gives you one success right away, and a nicely made bed is waiting for you at the end of each day.

Think about the rest of your day in sections as well. What do you do before you work? When do you take breaks? When do you eat? Consider these questions as you walk yourself through your day.

Once you have basic routines that take care of the little things, take a look at your long-term goals to come up with a daily system. Create your system based on what's right in front of you. Though you have goals, having a system is actually a better use of your time and productivity.

What is the Difference Between Goals and Systems?

Goals are important. They motivate us to become the people we are meant to be. They guide us through the storms of life by providing a light at the end of the tunnel. Goals determine our values and the way we live our lives. **We look at the future and the bigger picture of our life in the long-term when we set goals.**

Systems are also important. **Systems zoom in on the day-to-day and minute-to-minute details** on the actions that will bring your long-term goals to fruition.

However, if you spend all your time looking at the goal on the horizon, you might lose track of what is right in front of you. Instead of only focusing on the future, look at this exact moment. Look at each moment and the role it plays in propelling you to success.

In order to create your system in the most effective way, you must start by setting your goals. Big picture goals are based on the lifestyle and career paths that you want to pursue. Systems are the building blocks to those goals.

Follow this process to set long-term goals:

1. **Consider your values.** What do you consider "success"? Do you want to accumulate a fortune? Accolades? Community? Think about what your life will look like when you feel that you've reached your full potential.

2. **Zoom in on one aspect of your desired outcome.** For example, consider what job you would like to have. What kind of person do you want to be? Five years from now, what would you like to have accomplished?

3. **Time your goals realistically.** Think about how long it might take you to get to your goal. This will help you visualize your goal. Be careful not to take on too much. You want to set yourself up for success instead of disappointment.

Building a System

Once you have a long-term goal set in place, you'll be able to set up your day-to-day system. Break down your goal into six-month intervals. Next, break it into one-month intervals. Finally, think about the specific things you need to do on a daily or weekly basis to take constant steps toward the official destination.

Your system consists of the things you do and focus on daily that move you toward your long-term goal.

By creating your daily system, you'll be able to let go of the future and focus on enjoying the present moment. **You won't need to worry about your goal when you're following your system because success is built into each day.**

For example, imagine you have a goal to write a 300-page book in one year. What do you need to do each day to reach that goal? By breaking down each page into month sections, and taking one day off per week, you could realistically write 500 words per day. At what time of day would you write?

Build your system based on your long-term goal. When there's a long-term goal, the small steps support that goal. You don't need to keep your eyes on the prize. **You only need to keep your eyes on this present moment.** By doing this, you'll experience less stress and a greater likelihood of success.

The steps you take each day to work towards the finish line can be seamlessly placed throughout each part of your day. **Set up the rest of your day to reflect the goals you want to work towards.**

Set a Schedule, Stick to It

Lay out your entire day by creating a realistic schedule of your day-to-day system. In order to make the most effective use of your time and be the most productive, **map out the hour-to-hour details that comprise each of your days.**

Before you schedule anything, take a look at the way you're currently spending your time. **Take one week to observe each hour of your day.** Document the way you currently spend your time. This exercise will help you create a structure that can provide support and help you make the most use of your time with the least amount of stress.

An Example of a Schedule on a Typical Day

Time	Task
7:00 am - 8:00 am	✓ Wake up ✓ Make bed ✓ Meditate ✓ Eat breakfast
8:00 am - 9:00 am	✓ Go to work ✓ Review to-do list and priorities ✓ Check email
9:00 am - 12:00 pm	✓ Work on tasks in order of priority ✓ Take planned breaks at least every 90 minutes

Reduce the Scope

You don't need to do everything all in one day. **If you put too much on your plate, you'll wind up losing more time and producing less work.** Imagine a doctor who books too many patients in one day. If there's any disturbance in the schedule, the waiting room will grow more crowded as the wait gets longer.

Reduce the scope of your day and focus only on what is realistic. If you end up taking on too much, it will be harder to follow a schedule. *A full plate is a catalyst for stress and incomplete work.* Be quick, but don't hurry. Avoid overwhelming yourself in order to be efficient.

Leave No Task Untouched

Maintain the order of your day to the best of your ability. If you have a daily routine you want to follow, stick to it. **Follow the order of each event, even if you no longer have the planned amount of time.**

For example, if you planned to clean your house for an hour, but only have 20 minutes, you can focus on one room and get that done.

This habit will also help you maintain your daily schedule in the long run, even if it doesn't work on one day. Things may not be going as planned, but time can still be used wisely. Even though not everything was accomplished, the feeling of success will still come after doing everything that you could.

Batching

When you batch your days, you complete tasks that are similar to each other in sections. For example, you might have one hour on your schedule to check emails and return phone calls. You can split your days into sections and create a streamlined organization.

There seems to be a culture that encourages constant email-checking. **However, new research suggests checking email just three times per day.** For some, this sounds stressful. The fear of missing out comes into play, which makes checking email irresistible.

This habit is a difficult one to break. You can start small. Check your email five times per day. You can even let people know that all of their emails will be responded to within 24 hours.

Social media is a huge part of daily life for many people. It has become a natural way to communicate and connect with people within our community and throughout the world. Social media can also be as addicting as checking email.

A healthy habit to implement is one of conscious social media time. Rather than checking notifications every time there is a free moment, choose a time of day that you'll dedicate to social media.

Here are some examples of batching categories that may work well for your time management when you batch them together:

1. **Professional Correspondence**
   - Check email.
   - Return phone calls.
2. **Social Hour**
   - Check text messages.
   - Coordinate social plans.
   - Check social media.
3. **Current Events**
   - Check in on the news.
   - Get updates on topics of interest.
4. **Self-Improvement**
   - Go to the gym.
   - Work towards your long-term goal.

You can examine the rest of your schedule and look at your most productive time of day in order to choose where you batch which tasks. **Use your productivity time to your advantage and create a schedule according to which tasks need the most attention.**

There are even days of the week when you might want to take care of an entire category of tasks.

Theme Your Days

Some activities don't need to be done every day. For example, you might not need to go to the grocery store every day. Activities that can be put on just one day can be categorized into themes for your days. If you have multiple errands to do each week, choose just one day to do all of them.

These themes are part of your weekly rituals and habits that you want to maintain over time.

Whether you take your dog to the dog park once a week or choose one day each week to have meetings with coworkers, doing them on the same day each week will create a stable consistency.

Consider these suggested themes:

Mastery Mondays

- Practice a new hobby.
- Improve a new skill.

Productivity Tuesdays

- Complete big projects.
- Schedule meetings for this day.
- Dedicate extra focus to work.

Workout Wednesdays

- Schedule a longer workout session.
- Work with a professional trainer.

Thinking of your week in sections like this helps you focus on the day ahead, rather than the month or year ahead.

Make Time for Fun

Create time to pursue the things you love that are not work related. A great way to reward yourself after a satisfying, hard day of work is to engage in one of your hobbies. Productivity is essential. Embracing hobbies is also an essential way to avoid burnout.

When you've scheduled your day and prioritized your tasks, you'll be better able to make time for the things you love. **If you find that you have so much on your plate that you don't have time for fun, the solution is not to eliminate fun.**

Instead, start by carving out as little as one hour per week to dedicate to a hobby. Whether you enjoy deejayin, hiking, or Zumba, you can make time for both your high-priority responsibilities and your extracurricular hobbies.

It can be difficult to find hobbies as life takes over. Time flies by as the hustle and bustle determines how our days go. By taking charge and making positive changes in your time management skills, you'll suddenly find that you have more free time to dedicate to fostering a well-rounded lifestyle.

Short on fun? Use these techniques to choose a new hobby:

1. **Make a list.** Write down all the things you're interested in. You don't need to have an end plan in mind, just jot down the first things that come to mind. For example, you may be interested in astrology, painting, and filmmaking.

2. **Once you have a list of interests, choose a few to try out.** By exploring a new hobby, you'll broaden your horizons and have a stronger ability to approach work with a fresh outlook.

3. **Avoid limiting yourself.** You don't have to have just one hobby. You can pursue a number of things you're interested in. Just ensure that you don't take on too much.

The Bottom Line

Take inventory of your daily life and *let go of the habits that no longer serve you*. Acquiring new time management skills will foster a greater spark of productivity that will endure through the obstacles that naturally arise.

You don't have to expend energy and worry about the organization of your day. Regular practice and implementation of a few simple skills can actually save you time, so that you can better focus on what is pertinent to the current moment.

Follow this process to integrate effective time management skills into your daily routines:

Step 1: Begin by considering when you are most productive. Take stock of what your days currently look like and make realistic adjustments in order to use your time most effectively.

- Use your highest-alert times to take care of your highest-priority items. Schedule your meetings and free time according to the ebb and flow of your day.

- Create your ideal setting for productivity. **Think about *where* you feel the most comfortable.** Find an accessible and consistent setting where you can focus and get into the flow of your work day.

Step 2: Choose one task to focus on at a time. Let go of old multitasking habits that halt productivity, diminish work quality, and stir up more stress. Use strategies that will limit distractions. This will help you maintain focus.

- It takes around 25 minutes to refocus on a task once you've broken focus. Switching from task to task is unproductive and will end up wasting time. It's best to focus on each task as it comes.

- **Complete one task before moving on to the next.** A day with one complete project is more successful than a day with two incomplete projects.

Step 3: Examine the importance of each task ahead of you. Depending upon time constraints and level of focus, prioritize your tasks. Begin your work time with the most important task.

- Despite all of the planning in the world, many days go in a different direction than intended.

- **Remain flexible in the face of distraction or interruption.** Referring to your prioritized list can help you make decisions about how to use a limited amount of time.

Step 4: Be attentive of your time. Take care to notice how you spend each day. The day does not need to be daunting or overwhelming.

- **Planned mindfulness breaks will help the day go by at an even pace.** Take a step back after around 90 minutes of work time. In doing so, you'll be able to maintain a consistent work pace and quality of focus.

- **Follow a simple and consistent routine.** Think of your day in sections. Consider what each part of your day looks like, beginning with the moment you wake up.

Step 5: Develop and sustain an efficient system in which you will thrive. A system is created based on your long-term goals. Instead of constantly looking towards the future, bring your attention to what you can do each day that will inevitably lead to your goals.

- Goals are based on long-term, big picture ideas for your life.

- Systems are the small, daily steps that lead to achievement of those long-term goals.

Step 6: Create a schedule that works for you. Be careful not to take on more than you can handle.

- **Knowing your limits is good for you, good for your work, and good for the people around you.**
- If your daily schedule is disturbed, do your best to get to every task. If you planned an hour but only have 20 minutes, spend a focused, productive 20-minute period on the scheduled task.
- Categorize sections of your days based on the similarity of different tasks. If you have administrative tasks to do, do them all in the same part of your day.
- Spend less time checking your email. Schedule times to check your email and take care of those responses during planned parts of your day.
- **Pursue hobbies.** Making time for intentional fun ensures a consistent and stress-free quality of life. Though life may sometimes seem too busy for hobbies, you can make time for them when you implement effective time management skills.

Mindshift Conclusion

A natural consequence of time management is an increase in productivity. Distractions and worries are minimized when your days are predictable and simple. Consistent and regular practice of these time management tools are the catalysts for innovation and growth.

Final Encouragement
You Are on Your Way to Your Best You

☙

Use this book as a daily source of guidance. Make sure that you take it one Mindshift at a time. You don't want to overwhelm yourself with too much change all at once. The kind of work you are engaging in is very difficult to do; you are changing the momentum of your life for the better!

One key I want you to remember is that you *must* have patience with yourself as you begin to incorporate these Mindshifts into your life. This will be a moment-to-moment battle with the "old" you. Yes, it *will* be challenging to practice these Mindshifts consistently. There will be days where your growth will be tested, but remember you can make the decision from moment-to-moment to shift your thinking in the trajectory or success or failure; it is always your choice.

Keep your eye on the prize and love yourself, believe in yourself, and believe that you have all you need to live an absolutely happy and healthy life. The goal is to always become better than who you were yesterday.

Listen to the Emerge To Greatness Podcast here.
 https://emerge.buzzsprout.com or scan the QR Code below.

Pre-order your Emerge to Greatness t-shirt at
https://www.haynie.info/shop or scan the QR Code below.

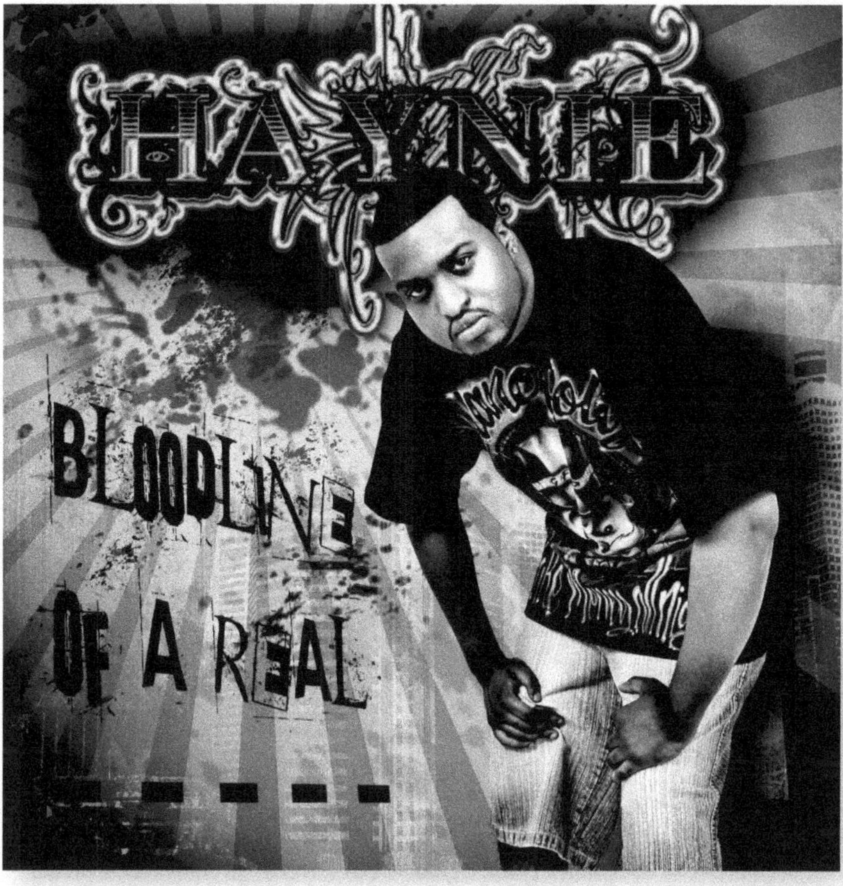

Go to link to purchase my album *Bloodline of a Real*

https://www.haynie.info/product-page/Haynie-Bloodline-Album-Purchase

or scan QR Code below.

www.ingramcontent.com/pod-product-compliance
Lightning Source LLC
Chambersburg PA
CBHW071504150426
43191CB00009B/1416